ALSACE

FRENCH REGIONAL COOKERY

ALSACE

Sebastien Badia

OCTOPUS BOOKS

Series consultant MARIE-PIERRE MOINE, editor of
TASTE magazine

Editor Diana Craig
Art Editor Lisa Tai
Copy editors Anne Johnson, Jenni Fleetwood
Designer Mike Leaman
Picture Researcher Gale Carlill
Production Controller Eleanor McCallum

Introduction written by Kate Whiteman
Translation of French material Madeleine Johnson,
Lesley Bernstein
Special Photography Jan Baldwin, Clive Streeter
Food Preparation Eve Dowling, Linda Fraser, Dolly
Meers, Lyn Rutherford
Styling Maria Kelly, Marion Price, Sue Russell

The publishers would like to thank the following for their
kind permission to reproduce the following photographs:
Topham Picture Library page 7;
Francis Jalain/Explorer page 9

Half-title page picture: Kügelhopf; title page picture:
Escargots à l'Alsacienne/Presskopf

First published in 1989 by Octopus Books Limited
a division of the Octopus Publishing Group
Michelin House
81 Fulham Road
London SW3 6RB

ISBN 0 7064 3102 2

Printed by Mandarin Offset in Hong Kong

CONTENTS

INTRODUCTION

Alsace is perhaps the most unusual and distinctive of the French provinces. Only the Rhine separates it from Germany and it has twice in its history belonged to that country, yet its people feel profoundly French and share the traditional French love of fine food and good living.

Historical background

Alsace has had a fascinating and eventful history. In mediaeval times, it was divided into a number of principalities, and Strasbourg and Colmar were granted the status of Imperial Cities by the Emperor Charlemagne. The region became very important: Martin Luther preached the Reformation there in the sixteenth century and the Peasant War followed. All this time, Alsace remained independent of any larger state or country, being incorporated into France only in 1648, under the Treaty of Westphalia. Even then its capital, Strasbourg, retained its independence for a further thirty-three years and Mulhouse in Upper Alsace remained free for more than another century, finally becoming French in 1798. The whole of Alsace was now French for the first time in its history, but the link was soon to be severed.

Less than 100 years later, France was forced to give up Alsace and parts of neighbouring Lorraine to the Germans after the Franco-Prussian war in 1871, and Alsace-Lorraine was created. Many Germans migrated into this new territory and brought with them their customs, architecture and language, which have remained features of the region to this day. A Germanic dialect is still spoken in parts of Alsace, which has always retained more of a German character than Lorraine.

Then came the First World War in 1914 and once again Alsace-Lorraine became part of France. The people of Alsace might now have hoped to stay French for ever, but Europe was again torn by war and, in 1940, the province was once more incorporated into Germany. This time it remained German for another five years until the end of the Second World War. Strasbourg, the capital, was liberated at the end of 1944, but the beautiful old town of Colmar continued under German occupation until 1945. In 1949, Strasbourg became the home of the Council of Europe and its chequered territorial history ceased, leaving Alsace firmly French but probably suffering from a slight identity crisis after two periods of French domination and two of German!

Geography of the region

Alsace is split into three distinct zones: the plains, the mountainous Vosges, and their lower slopes. The plains, bounded by the Rhine, are dotted with picturesque villages, each with its own tall church spire and typical half-timbered and steep-roofed houses. The fertile land here is used for the cultivation of grains and vegetables, while in the south this gives way to the growing of hops, from which the delicious local beer is made.

At the foot of the Vosges lie the vineyards which produce the famous wines of Alsace, while the Vosges themselves, which divide Alsace from Lorraine, are scattered with mountain pastures where sheep and cows graze.

Food

With all this geographical and historical richness, it is not surprising that the food of Alsace is excellent and varied. The German influence is very strong, perhaps most obviously in the abundance of *charcuterie*. The Alsations refer affectionately to their pigs as *'seigneur cochon'* (Lord Pig) and every tiny village takes immense pride in its hams, sausages and terrines. There is salt pork, too, black puddings and every kind of pâté.

Most famous of all the regional specialities is *choucroûte*, the French version of the German *sauerkraut* – cabbage pickled in salt and usually served with fat smoked sausages. Almost every brasserie serves the dish with its local beer and there are even *choucroûte* festivals.

The freshwater fish from the Rhine are renowned, too, and play a major role in the cooking of the region. Salmon and trout are abundant and white fish, such as eel, pike, tench and bream are stewed in Alsation wine to make a *matelote*.

Right *A peaceful riverside scene, showing typical half-timbered Alsatian houses overhanging the water*

There are fine local cheeses, too, the most famous being Munster, which has been made in the region for centuries. The mediaeval monks originally made this cheese, which is mild when young and gradually matures to a rich, sweet flavour; its name is a corruption of the Latin *monasterium*. Cheeses are often used to make quiches, the best-known being quiche Lorraine.

Alsation geese are famous for their delicate flesh, but above all for their specially fattened livers (*foies gras*) for which Strasbourg, in particular, is justly famous. Every restaurant serves its own version of those unctuous livers, in slivers or scoops, or made into a pâté.

The strong Jewish influence which pervades Alsace is much in evidence in the region's cuisine; the old-established Jewish settlers brought traditional recipes from Poland, Austria and Russia as well as Germany. One example of this is the Alsatian love of goose meat, which is served in every conceivable manner, from stuffed necks to stewed gizzards and is often accompanied by inelegant-looking but delicious *spätzele* noodles.

The Jewish and German influence is also found in the patisserie of Alsace. Cream from the well-fattened cows, jams from the magnificent local fruits (in particular golden *mirabelle* and greengage-like *quetsche* plums) and pastry made from the wheat which grows on the plains all combine to make rich, sweet pastries and tarts, *kügelhopf*, *lebkuchen* and almondy *Linzertorte*.

Wines

To accompany all these riches, there are, of course, the wines of Alsace, whose fruitiness and fragrance set them apart from other French wines, although, not surprisingly, they do resemble the German wines which are made from the grapes which grow further along the Rhine.

The wine-growing region of Alsace is exceptionally pretty, with the spectacular Vosges mountains on one side and the beautiful Rhine valley on the other. Despite its northerly location, the vineyards are well sheltered and enjoy plenty of sunshine and one of the lowest levels of rainfall in France; indeed, Colmar is the driest town in France after the much more southerly Perpignan. The winters are cold, however, so the vines start growing late and the grapes are left to ripen in the hot dry summer, to be harvested late in October.

The resulting wines have a special, aromatic fla-vour, with a touch of spiciness. Even their appearance is distinctive; they come in slim, stylish bottles which are exclusive to the region by law. The law also requires that the wine be bottled where it is produced, which guarantees its authenticity.

While most French wines are named after their place of origin, Alsation wines are usually named after the grapes from which they are made – thus there is Gewürztraminer, Riesling, Pinot Blanc, Sylvaner and Muscat, which all produce white wines, Pinot Gris (rosé) and Pinot Noir (red). The most full-bodied of the whites is Gewürztraminer (whose name means 'spicy'). Many people consider Riesling to be the best of all the wines of Alsace, with its fragrant bouquet and fruity aftertaste. Both these wines make a superb accompaniment to game, *foie gras* or indeed any other Alsatian food.

Sylvaner is a lighter wine, with a less sweet fragrance, while Pinot Blanc is crisp and fresh. Muscat has a heavy, sweet bouquet which somewhat belies its dry, clean taste. In Alsace, it is often drunk as an apertif, but it also goes well with fish. Another popular regional variation is Crémant D'Alsace, a sparkling wine produced in the Champagne manner. All Alsace white wines are drunk young and are traditionally served lightly chilled, in tall green-stemmed glasses – an appropriate vessel for their delicate yellow colour.

Alsatian rosé and red wines are less distinguished than the whites, although the Gentil, made from the Pinot Noir grape, does resemble a Burgundy. It is drunk with the game which abounds in the area and with beef and lamb. Never tell a native of Alsace that his wine is not as good as that of another region, though! The people are fiercely proud of their province, and justly so. Having been shuttled back and forth between France and Germany for so many years, they have evolved their own special style and have a fierce regional patriotism. If you go to Alsace and manifestly enjoy its splendours – natural, architectural, gastronomic and vinous – you will be assured of the warmest possible welcome.

Right *A baker bears a tray laden with* kügelhopf, *a sweet bread and a particular speciality of the region*

SOUPS

Like much of the region's cuisine, Alsatian soups tend to be robust, substantial affairs, ideal for a cold winter's night. Many of them, like *Soupe de Lentilles aux Saucisses* or the classic *Soup à l'Oignon Gratinée*, are filling enough to make a meal in their own right, with perhaps only a salad, some crusty bread and a bottle of wine as accompaniment.

CRÈME DE GRENOUILLES AU CERFEUIL
CREAM OF FROGS' LEGS' SOUP WITH CHERVIL

SERVES 6
450 g (1 lb) frogs' legs
50 g (2 oz) shallots, peeled and chopped
6 tablespoons dry white wine
750 ml (1¼ pints) fish stock
750 ml (1¼ pints) water
100 g (4 oz) carrots, peeled and chopped
100 g (4 oz) leeks, chopped
100 g (4 oz) celery, chopped
100 g (4 oz) butter
300 ml (½ pint) single cream
salt and pepper
2 tablespoons chopped chervil

1 Place the frogs' legs in a pan with the shallots, white wine, fish stock and water. Bring to the boil and simmer gently for 20 minutes.

2 Lift the frogs' legs out of the pan with a slotted spoon. Remove the bones, reserving the flesh for use later. Return the bones to the pan and simmer for another 15 minutes.

3 Strain the stock to remove the bones and shallots and put to one side.

4 Cook the vegetables in 75 g (3 oz) of the butter, over a very gentle heat. Add the prepared stock and the cream, and bring to the boil. Reduce by one third. Check the seasoning, adding salt and pepper as necessary, and whisk in the remaining butter. Stir in the reserved flesh from the frogs' legs and the chopped chervil.

SOUPE DE LENTILLES AUX SAUCISSES
LENTIL SOUP WITH SAUSAGES

SERVES 6 TO 8
100 g (4 oz) carrots, peeled and finely chopped
100 g (4 oz) leeks, finely chopped
65 g (2½ oz) celery, finely chopped
1 tablespoon butter or goose fat
1 clove garlic, peeled and crushed
200 g (7 oz) green or brown lentils, soaked overnight
1.7 litres (3 pints) chicken stock
100 g (4 oz) potatoes, peeled and diced
salt and pepper
6 Strasbourg sausages, sliced

1 Fry the carrots, leeks and celery in the fat. Add the garlic and lentils, and cover with stock. Bring to the boil, skim off any scum and simmer gently for 30 minutes.

2 Add the potatoes, season with salt and pepper and simmer for another 10 minutes.

3 Check the seasoning, add the sausages and serve.

CRÈME DE GRENOUILLES AU CERFEUIL *(ABOVE)*
VELOUTÉ À LA BIÈRE ET CROÛTONS FRITS
(BELOW, RECIPE PAGE 13)

SOUPE DE LENTILLES AUX SAUCISSES *(RECIPE PAGE 10)*

SOUPE AUX CHOUX FRISÉS ET LARDONS
CABBAGE SOUP WITH BACON

SERVES 6
1 small curly cabbage, shredded
1 tablespoon vinegar
200 g (7 oz) smoked bacon, diced
75 g (3 oz) goose fat or butter
100 g (4 oz) carrots, peeled and finely diced
100 g (4 oz) leeks, finely diced
50 g (2 oz) celery, finely diced
1.5 litres (2½ pints) chicken stock
salt and pepper
100 g (4 oz) potatoes, peeled and diced

1 Wash the cabbage in water acidulated with vinegar.

2 Fry the bacon gently in goose fat or butter. Add the cabbage, carrots, leeks and celery and stew gently, covered, for 5 minutes.

3 Add the stock, season with salt and pepper and simmer for 20 minutes. Add the potatoes and simmer for another 10 minutes. Serve very hot.

VELOUTÉ À LA BIÈRE ET CROÛTONS FRITS
CREAM OF BEER SOUP WITH CROÛTONS

SERVES 6
100 g (4 oz) onions, peeled and finely sliced
100 g (4 oz) butter
50 g (2 oz) plain flour
300 ml (½ pint) light beer or lager
1 litre (1¾ pints) chicken stock
3 slices brown bread
6 tablespoons single cream
salt and pepper
1 tablespoon chopped chervil

1 Fry the onions in half the butter until golden brown. Add the flour and continue to cook until lightly coloured. Add the beer, stirring well, then add the stock and bring to the boil. Simmer for 25 minutes.

2 Cut the bread into cubes and fry in the remaining butter until golden brown. Drain on kitchen towels and keep warm.

3 Strain the soup or purée in an electric blender. Bring back to the boil, add the cream and simmer for another 5 minutes. Season and add the chervil. Serve with *croûtons*.

CRÈME DE GIBIER AUX CROÛTONS
CREAM OF GAME SOUP WITH CROÛTONS

SERVES 6 TO 8
200 g (7 oz) game, such as pheasant (boned weight), roughly chopped
500 g (1¼ lb) game trimmings
1 kg (2¼ lb) veal bones, finely chopped
6 tablespoons oil
100 g (4 oz) leeks, finely chopped
100 g (4 oz) carrots, peeled and finely chopped
100 g (4 oz) celeriac, peeled and finely chopped
100 g (4 oz) green cabbage, finely chopped
50 g (2 oz) onions, peeled and finely chopped
2 cloves garlic, peeled and crushed
2 pinches of thyme
1 bay leaf
2 cloves
100 g (4 oz) plain flour
6 tablespoons dry white wine
2 litres (3½ pints) water
300 ml (½ pint) cream
4 large slices bread, cut into cubes
50 g (2 oz) butter

1 Fry the game meat, trimmings and veal bones in the oil in a large flameproof casserole. Add the vegetables, garlic, herbs and cloves. Stir in the flour and cook until slightly coloured. Stir in the wine and water.

2 Bring to the boil and simmer for 1½ hours. Discard the meat and bones. Pass through a sieve and return to the pan. Bring back to the boil and simmer for at least 5 minutes.

3 Fry the bread in butter. Add the cream to the soup and bring back to the boil. Serve with the *croûtons*.

CONSOMMÉ DE BOEUF AUX QUENELLES DE MOELLE
BEEF CONSOMMÉ WITH MARROW DUMPLINGS

SERVES 6
150 g (5 oz) beef marrow
2 eggs
100 g (4 oz) breadcrumbs
20 g (¾ oz) plain flour
75 g (3 oz) chervil and parsley, finely chopped
salt and pepper
grated nutmeg
100 g (4 oz) vermicelli
1.2 litres (2 pints) beef stock

1 Beat the marrow with the eggs, breadcrumbs, flour, chervil and parsley. Season with salt, pepper and grated nutmeg. Alternatively, you can use an electric blender to mix these ingredients.

2 Cook the vermicelli in salted boiling water. Bring the consommé to the boil.

3 Shape the marrow mixture into small balls and poach in the simmering consommé for 10 minutes. Serve very hot, garnished with vermicelli.

SOUPE D'ESCARGOTS À L'OSEILLE
SNAIL AND SORREL SOUP

SERVES 6
36 snails, removed from tin and drained
100 g (4 oz) butter
50 g (2 oz) onions, peeled and chopped
25 g (1 oz) plain flour
6 tablespoons dry white wine
200 g (7 oz) sorrel, roughly chopped
100 g (4 oz) carrots, peeled and chopped
100 g (4 oz) leeks, chopped
1.5 litres (2½ pints) chicken stock
salt and pepper

1 Lightly fry the snails in half the butter. Add the onions and fry for a little longer, until the onions are soft but not brown. Stir in the flour and cook for 1 minute. Deglaze with white wine and put to one side.

2 Lightly fry the sorrel, carrots and leeks in the remaining butter until soft. Add the stock, season with salt and pepper and simmer for 20 minutes. Sieve the soup or purée in an electric blender.

3 Add the snails and their juices to the soup. Simmer for 5 minutes. Check the seasoning and serve.

CRÈME D'ASPERGES
CREAM OF ASPARAGUS SOUP

SERVES 6
500 g (1¼ lb) asparagus, trimmed
a few drops of lemon juice
2 pinches of sugar
50 g (2 oz) celery, sliced
50 g (2 oz) leek, sliced
75 g (3 oz) butter
50 g (2 oz) flour
1.5 litres (2½ pints) chicken stock
200 ml (⅓ pint) single cream
salt and pepper

1 Cut off the asparagus tips and cook in boiling water, lightly acidulated with lemon juice and sweetened with 1 pinch of sugar, for 5 to 10 minutes, keeping the tips slightly firm.

2 Chop the asparagus stems and sweat gently with the celery and leek. Stew, covered, for 5 minutes, then add the flour, stock and 1 pinch of sugar.

3 Simmer the soup for 20 minutes. Sieve or work in the liquidizer. Add the cream, salt and pepper, and reduce by one third.

4 Dice the cooked asparagus tips and use to garnish the soup. Serve immediately.

SOUPE D'ESCARGOTS À L'OSEILLE *(ABOVE)*
CONSOMMÉ DE BEOUF AUX QUENELLES
DE MOELLE *(BELOW)*

SOUPE À L'OIGNON GRATINÉE

SOUPE À L'OIGNON GRATINÉE
GRATINÉED ONION SOUP

SERVES 6
500 g (1¼ lb) onions, peeled and finely sliced
75 g (3 oz) butter
50 g (2 oz) plain flour
6 tablespoons dry white wine, such as Sylvaner
1.5 litres (2½ pints) chicken stock
2 pinches of thyme
1 bay leaf
salt and pepper
12-18 slices French stick
200 g (7 oz) Gruyère, grated

1 Brown the onions in butter. Add the flour and cook for a few more minutes until just golden brown. Add the wine, stock and herbs. Season with salt and pepper and simmer for 15 minutes.

2 Toast the slices of bread. Check the seasoning of the soup and pour into bowls. Place 2 to 3 slices of toast on top of each bowl and sprinkle with grated cheese. Place the bowls under a hot grill for 2 to 3 minutes to brown the cheese.

SOUPE AUX ABATTIS D'OIE À LA MÉNAGÈRE
GOOSE GIBLET SOUP

This soup is traditionally made from goose giblets, but turkey giblets may be used instead. The feet are necessary for the gelatinous quality they provide.

SERVES 6 TO 8
giblets from 2 geese or turkeys (including feet), cleaned
50 g (2 oz) butter
2 carrots, peeled and finely diced
2 leeks (white part only), sliced
50 g (2 oz) celery, finely sliced
3 litres (5½ pints) water
bouquet garni
salt and pepper
100 g (4 oz) long-grain rice
grated nutmeg
chopped chervil, to garnish

1 Prepare the giblets. Singe the neck, the head and the pinions and carefully remove all feathers. Scald the feet by plunging into boiling water, peel off the outer skin and cut off the ends of the spurs. Cut a shallow slit along the curved side of the gizzard, taking care not to penetrate the inner sac. Remove the inner sac and discard. Remove the gall bladder from the liver and trim off the upper part of the heart. Cut all the giblets into small pieces. Place in a saucepan and cover with boiling water, then drain.

2 Melt the butter in a saucepan. Add the vegetables and sauté over gentle heat for about 5 minutes. Add the water, giblets, bouquet garni and salt and pepper. Bring to the boil and simmer for about 1½ hours, skimming off any scum. Remove excess fat.

3 Stir in the rice and simmer for 30 minutes more. Remove the bouquet garni, check the seasoning and add grated nutmeg to taste. Serve garnished with chervil.

SOUPE À LA CRÈME (PANADE)
CREAM SOUP WITH PANADA

SERVES 6
6 slices (about 200 g/7 oz) day-old white bread, crusts removed
1.5 litres (2½ pints) chicken stock
1 egg
300 ml (1½ pint) single cream
25 g (1 oz) butter
salt and pepper
grated nutmeg
milk (optional)

1 Cut the bread into cubes and place in a large saucepan with the stock. Bring to the boil and simmer for 15 minutes, stirring occasionally. Whisk to a smooth purée.

2 Beat the egg with the cream in a small bowl. Stir in 2 tablespoons of the hot soup, then gradually add this mixture to the saucepan, whisking constantly. Whisk in the butter. Add salt and pepper and nutmeg to taste. If the soup is too thick, add a little milk. Serve hot.

Alsatian cuisine achieves some of its greatest triumphs in its terrines, pâtés and pressed meats, the most celebrated of course being *pâté de foie gras*. Here, it is encased in a hot-water pastry crust, and pastry features again in the recipes for some of Alsace's savoury tarts, like the creamy *Tarte à l'Oignon* below. Finally, to complete the chapter, there are two recipes for snails and two for cold, marinated fish.

TOURTE DE CAILLES AUX RAISINS
QUAIL PIE WITH GRAPES

SERVES 6
6 quail, boned
3 tablespoons white wine
50 g (2 oz) shallots, peeled and sliced
25 g (1 oz) *fines herbes* (such as chives, parsley, chervil), finely chopped
25 g (1 oz) butter
450 g (1 lb) chicken meat (boned weight)
salt and pepper
grated nutmeg
2 eggs
100 ml (4 fl oz) single cream
150 g (5 oz) Pâte Brisée (see page 77)
75 g (3 oz) grapes, peeled and seeded
100 g (4 oz) Pâte Feuilletée (see page 77)

1 Marinate the quail breasts overnight in white wine with shallots and *fines herbes*.

2 The following day, remove from the marinade and fry quickly in butter. Allow to cool.

3 Mince the chicken and the brown quail meat. Season with salt, pepper and nutmeg, and add 2 of the eggs and the cream.

4 Line a buttered 18 cm (7 inch) round pie dish with shortcrust pastry so that the edge overlaps the edge of the dish. Add half the prepared filling and, on top of this, arrange the quail breasts and grapes. Cover with the remaining filling. Bring the shortcrust pastry edge back over the top and cover with a flaky pastry lid. Seal the pastry, brush with beaten egg and decorate with a fork.

5 Bake in a moderately hot oven at 200°C (400°F), Gas Mark 6. After 15 minutes, lower the temperature to 150°C (300°F), Gas Mark 2, and bake for another 40 minutes. The pie is cooked when a skewer plunged into it comes out warm. Serve warm with a green salad.

TARTE À L'OIGNON (ZEWELWAÏ)
ONION TART

SERVES 6
100 g (4 oz) smoked bacon, diced
500 g (1¼ lb) onions, peeled and finely sliced
50 g (2 oz) butter
25 g (1 oz) plain flour
200 ml (⅓ pint) milk
6 tablespoons single cream
2 egg yolks
salt and pepper
grated nutmeg
250 g (9 oz) Pâte Brisée (see page 77)

1 Fry the bacon and onion gently in butter until soft. Add the flour and stir in the milk and cream. Cook for 5 minutes. Take off the heat and add the egg yolks, salt, pepper and nutmeg. Allow to cool.

2 Line a buttered 25 cm (10 inch) flan tin with shortcrust pastry. Prick the bottom with a fork and fill with the prepared onion mixture. Bake in a moderate oven at 180°C (350°F), Gas Mark 4 for 40 minutes. Serve hot.

TARTE À L'OIGNON

TOURTE VIGNERONNE
PORK AND VEAL PIE

SERVES 8
450 g (1 lb) pork
450 g (1 lb) veal
100 g (4 oz) shallots, peeled and sliced
1 clove garlic, crushed
100 g (4 oz) parsley, chopped
1 pinch of thyme
1 bay leaf
grated nutmeg
200 ml (⅓ pint) white wine
350 ml (12 fl oz) single cream
250 g (9 oz) Pâte Brisée (see page 77)
3 eggs

1 Mince half the meats and dice the remainder finely. Mix with the shallots, garlic, parsley, thyme, bay leaf, salt, pepper and nutmeg. Cover with wine and 6 tablespoons of cream, and leave to marinate overnight in the refrigerator.

2 Line a buttered 25 cm (10 inch) flan tin with shortcrust pastry. Fill with the marinated mixture and cover with a pastry lid. Seal the edges, make a hole in the centre to allow the steam to escape, and brush with beaten egg, using 1 of the eggs.

3 Bake in a moderately hot oven at 200°C (400°F), Gas Mark 6. After 15 minutes, lower the temperature to 180°C (350°F), Gas Mark 4 and bake for another 30 minutes.

4 Mix the 2 remaining eggs with the rest of the cream and season with salt, pepper and nutmeg. Pour this mixture into the pie through the air vent in the centre and bake for another 10 to 15 minutes until the pastry is golden brown. Serve immediately while still piping hot. The *tourte* may be accompanied by a green salad.

TERRINE DE FOIES DE VOLAILLE
CHICKEN LIVER PÂTÉ

FILLS A 1.1 LITRE (2 PINT) TERRINE
300 g (11 oz) chicken livers
750 g (1½ lb) veal and pork
6 tablespoons white wine
50 g (2 oz) shallots, peeled and chopped
1 pinch of thyme
2 bay leaves
1 pinch each of ground ginger, cloves,
cinnamon and nutmeg
2 eggs
salt and pepper
6 tablespoons single cream
250 g (9 oz) thinly sliced smoked bacon, rinded
100 g (4 oz) streaky bacon

1 Marinate the chicken livers, veal and pork overnight in white wine with the shallots, thyme, 1 bay leaf and spices.

2 Mince the meat and half the chicken livers. Add the eggs, season lightly with salt and pepper, and add the cream.

3 Fry the remaining chicken livers and allow to cool.

4 Line a 1.1 litre (2 pint) terrine with rashers of smoked bacon, arranging them so that they overlap the edges of the terrine. Add a layer of the prepared pâté mixture. Wrap the fried chicken livers in rashers of streaky bacon, forming a fat sausage the length of the terrine. Place in the terrine and cover with another layer of the pâté mixture. Press lightly and fold the bacon lining the terrine back over the top. Place 1 bay leaf on top of the bacon, and place in a shallow dish with enough hot water to come halfway up the sides of the terrine. Bake in a moderately hot oven, at 200°C (400°F), Gas Mark 6. After 15 minutes, lower the temperature to 150°C (300°F), Gas Mark 2, cover and bake for another 40 minutes.

5 Take out of the oven and allow to cool, covered with a plate with a weight on top to press evenly. Chill for 24 hours.

TOURTE VIGNERONNE *(ABOVE)*
TERRINE DE FOIES DE VOLAILLE *(BELOW)*

PÂTÉ DE FOIE GRAS EN CROÛTE *(ABOVE)*
TERRINE DE FOIE GRAS AU RIESLING *(BELOW)*

PÂTÉ DE FOIE GRAS EN CROÛTE
FOIE GRAS PÂTÉ IN PASTRY

FILLS a 900 G (2 LB) LOAF TIN
500 g (1¼ lb) fresh *foie gras* (fattened goose or
duck liver)
salt and pepper
3 tablespoons brandy
300 g (11 oz) lean pork
300 g (11 oz) veal
3 tablespoons Gewürztraminer Marc
1 pinch of thyme
1 bay leaf
1 pinch of ground nutmeg
2 eggs
6 tablespoons single cream
450 g (1 lb) Pâte à Pâtés en Croûte (see page 77)
GELÉE:
250 ml (8 fl oz) beef stock
4 leaves gelatine (or 2 tablespoons)
3 tablespoons Riesling

1 Remove the skin and any gristle from the liver. Season with salt and pepper and marinate overnight in brandy. Roughly dice the meats and marinate overnight in Marc with the thyme, bay leaf and nutmeg.

2 The following day, mince the pork and veal together, stir in 1 egg, salt, pepper and cream.

3 Line a 900 g (2 lb) loaf tin with the hot-water crust pastry and add half the prepared pâté mixture. Roll the liver in aluminium foil to shape it into a fat sausage the length of the tin. Remove the foil and arrange the liver in the tin. Cover with the remaining pâté mixture.

4 Cover with a pastry lid and seal the edges together with your fingers. Make two holes in the lid to allow steam to escape, brush with beaten egg and decorate with a fork.

5 Bake in a moderately hot oven for 10 minutes, at 200°C (400°F), Gas Mark 6, to set and brown the pastry. Then lower the temperature to 140°C (275°F), Gas Mark 1, and bake for another 40 minutes. The pâté is cooked when any fat appearing through the air vents is clear. Remove from the oven and allow to cool, covered with a plate with a weight on top.

6 To make the *geleé*, dissolve the gelatine in a little cold water. Bring the stock to the boil, add the gelatine and bring back to the boil. Pour into a bowl and, when lukewarm, stir in the Riesling. When the pâté is cold, pour a little liquid *gelée* on top and chill overnight.

TERRINE DE FOIE GRAS AU RIESLING
FOIE GRAS PÂTÉ WITH RIESLING

FILLS A 1½ LITRE (2½ PINT) TERRINE
1 kg (2¼ lb) fresh *foie gras* (fattened goose or
duck liver)
salt and white pepper
200 ml (⅓ pint) Riesling
300 ml (½ pint) Gelée (see previous recipe)

1 Separate the two halves of the livers, discarding the skin and any gristle. Place in a 1½ litre (2½ pint) terrine and season with salt and pepper. Pour over the Riesling and leave to marinate in the refrigerator overnight.

2 The following day, cover the terrine with a double thickness of greaseproof paper and secure with string. Place the terrine in a shallow dish with enough hot water to reach halfway up the sides of the terrine. Bake in a moderate oven, at 170°C (325°F), Gas Mark 3, for about 1½ hours. The liver is cooked when a skewer plunged into it comes out warm.

3 Remove the terrine from the dish of hot water. Allow to cool, covered with a plate with a weight on top to press the pâté and squeeze out any fat. When it is cold, pour the liquid aspic jelly on top and chill for 24 hours.

4 Serve the following day with a slice of grilled Kügelhopf (see page 69), cubes of aspic jelly and a little green salad. At the last moment, sprinkle the pâté with freshly ground pepper.

HARENGS MARINÉS
SOUSED HERRING

SERVES 6
6 salt herring
2 medium onions, sliced and separated into
rings
1 small carrot, finely chopped
1 bay leaf
12 whole black peppercorns
MARINADE:
1 tablespoon Dijon mustard
2 tablespoons oil
1 tablespoon red wine vinegar
250 ml (¼ pint) *crème fraîche*, or soured cream
salt and pepper

1 Arrange the herring in a single layer in a shallow dish. Pour over cold water to cover and set aside for 48 hours to remove the excess salt. Change the water several times.

2 Fillet, skin and trim the herring. Layer the fillets in a deep serving dish with the onions and carrot. Tuck the bay leaf between them and add the peppercorns.

3 Combine the mustard, oil and vinegar in a jug. Mix well. Whisk in the cream and add salt and pepper to taste. Spoon the mixture over the herring, cover and marinate for 48 hours in a cool place before serving, with boiled potatoes if liked.

FILETS DE SANDRE MARINÉS AU SYLVANER ET CITRON
PERCH MARINATED IN SYLVANER AND LEMON JUICE

SERVES 6
1.5 kg (3 lb) perch or pike fillet
450 g (1 lb) coarse sea salt
100 ml (4 fl oz) Sylvaner
150 ml (5 fl oz) lemon juice
150 ml (5 fl oz) olive oil
100 g (4 oz) shallots, chopped
2 lemons, peeled and quartered
1 large tomato, diced
8 sprigs chervil

1 Macerate the fish in sea salt for 3 hours. Rinse under cold running water for 5 minutes and dry.

2 Place in a shallow dish with the white wine, lemon juice, olive oil and chopped shallots, and leave to marinate for 18 hours.

3 Remove the fish from the marinade and cut into thin slices. Garnish with lemon quarters, diced tomato and sprigs of chervil. Serve with a green salad.

FRICASSÉE D'ESCARGOTS AUX HERBES
SNAIL FRICASSÉE WITH HERBS

SERVES 6
36 snails, removed from tin and drained
50 g (2 oz) butter
25 g (1 oz) shallots, peeled and chopped
50 g (2 oz) carrots, peeled and diced
50 g (2 oz) leeks, chopped
50 g (2 oz) celery, chopped
4 tablespoons white wine
120 ml (4 fl oz) chicken stock
4 tablespoons single cream
salt and pepper
50 g (2 oz) *fines herbes*, including parsley,
chervil and chives, chopped

1 Fry the snails in the butter. Add the shallots, carrots, leeks and celery. Deglaze with white wine.

2 Add the stock and boil for 2 minutes. Add the cream and season with salt and pepper. Add the herbs and stir in the remaining butter. Serve very hot.

HARENGS MARINÉS

ESCARGOTS À L'ALSACIENNE *(ABOVE)*
PRESSKOPF ALSACIEN *(BELOW)*

ESCARGOTS À L'ALSACIENNE
SNAILS ALSACE-STYLE

SERVES 6
36 snails and shells
150 g (5 oz) butter
3 tablespoons white wine
100 ml (4 fl oz) chicken stock
25 g (1 oz) garlic, peeled and crushed
50 g (2 oz) parsley, finely chopped
50 g (2 oz) shallots, peeled and finely chopped
50 g (2 oz) hazelnuts, crushed
salt and pepper

1 Remove the snails from the tin and fry in 25 g (1 oz) of the butter.

2 Deglaze with white wine and add the stock. Boil for 2 minutes and allow to cool. Remove the snails from the stock (this may be reserved and used as the basis for other sauces).

3 Cream the remaining butter and mix in the garlic, chopped parsley and shallots and the hazelnuts. Season with salt and pepper.

4 Put a knob of the flavoured butter in each snail shell, replace the snail and cover with a little more butter.

5 Arrange all the shells on snail dishes or, if these are unavailable, any other suitable ovenproof dish. Bake the snails in a moderately hot oven, at 200°C (400°F), Gas Mark 6, for 10 minutes. Serve very hot.

PRESSKOPF ALSACIEN
POTTED PORK

SERVES 6 TO 8
1 pig's head, split down the middle
2 pig's trotters, split in two
300 ml (½ pint) white wine
300 g (11 oz) carrots, peeled and roughly chopped
200 g (7 oz) celeriac, peeled and roughly chopped
200 g (7 oz) leeks, roughly chopped
200 g (7 oz) gherkins, chopped
MARINADE:
5 cloves garlic, peeled
5 cloves
1 onion, peeled and sliced
3 bay leaves
1 sprig thyme
6 juniper berries
10 peppercorns
25 g (1 oz) coarse salt

1 Put the pig's head and trotters in a deep dish, cover with the marinade ingredients, and marinate in the refrigerator for 2 days.

2 Put the pig's head and trotters in a large pan, cover with cold water and bring to the boil. Skim off any scum as it rises.

3 Pour the contents of the pan into a sieve and wash carefully under cold running water. Return to the well-rinsed pan, cover with cold water and add the white wine. Bring to the boil and skim off any scum. Add the vegetables and simmer for 2 hours until the meat comes away from the bones.

4 Lift the meat out of the pan and take off the bones. Dice the meat and strain the juices through a sieve. Place the meat in a 1.2 litre (2 pint) terrine, add the gherkins and stir. Pour the juices over the meat to cover completely. Leave in the refrigerator for 24 hours.

5 To serve, unmould the terrine and cut into slices. Serve with *crudités*.

SALADS

The salads in this chapter are not accompaniments to other dishes, but dishes in their own right, to be eaten at the beginning of a meal. Some, like *Salade de Pissenlits*, are crisp and light warm-weather refreshers; others – like *Salade de Lentilles Tiède* or *Salade de Pommes de Terre et Harengs à l'Huile* – are more hearty affairs and could easily form the basis of a light lunch or supper on their own.

SALADE DE BETTERAVES AUX NOIX
BEETROOT SALAD WITH WALNUTS

SERVES 6 TO 8
1 kg (2¼ lb) cooked beetroot, peeled and sliced
200 g (7 oz) onions, peeled and finely sliced
200 ml (⅓ pint) vinegar
200 ml (⅓ pint) walnut oil
salt and pepper
100 g (4 oz) fresh walnuts, shelled, peeled and halved
4 tablespoons chopped parsley

1 Mix the beetroot and onions, add the vinegar, oil, salt and pepper and marinate in the refrigerator for 2 hours.

2 Sprinkle the walnuts and parsley on top and serve.

SALADE DE GRUYÈRE
GRUYÈRE SALAD

SERVES 6
600 g (1¼ lb) Gruyère
Sauce Vinaigrette (see Salade de Pissenlits) with the addition of a few chopped spring onions

1 Cut the Gruyère into *bâtonnets* or short strips, 2 to 3 cm (1 to 1¼ inches) long, and 0.5 cm (¼ inch) thick.

2 Toss in the vinaigrette, arrange on a shallow dish and serve.

SALADE DE LENTILLES TIÈDE
WARM LENTIL SALAD

SERVES 6 TO 8
350 g (12 oz) green lentils, soaked for 3 to 4 hours
1 carrot, peeled
1 onion, peeled
1 pinch of thyme
1 bay leaf
1 clove
1 clove garlic, peeled
1 carrot, peeled and chopped
1 leek, chopped
100 g (4 oz) celery, chopped
200 g (7 oz) smoked streaky bacon, diced
1 tablespoon chopped chives
SAUCE VINAIGRETTE:
200 ml (⅓ pint) walnut oil
6 tablespoons sherry or wine vinegar
1 tablespoon Dijon mustard
salt and pepper

1 Drain the lentils. Place the lentils with the carrot, onion, thyme, bay leaf, clove and garlic in a saucepan and cover with cold water. Bring to the boil and cook for 30 to 35 minutes. Remove the vegetables, bay leaf and garlic, and drain the lentils.

2 Blanch the chopped vegetables in lightly salted boiling water.

3 Whisk the vinaigrette ingredients together. Fry the bacon until crisp. Add to the lentils and stir in the blanched vegetables and the vinaigrette. Sprinkle with chives and serve warm.

SALADE DE BETTERAVES AUX NOIX *(ABOVE)*
SALADE DE LENTILLES TIÈDE *(BELOW)*

SALADE DE CHOUCROUTE À L'HUILE DE NOIX
SAUERKRAUT SALAD WITH WALNUT OIL

SERVES 6 TO 8

750 g (1½ lb) sauerkraut, cooked in stock or water and drained
200 ml (⅓ pint) walnut oil
6 tablespoons vinegar
salt and pepper
150 g (5 oz) onions, peeled and finely chopped
50 g (2 oz) parsley, chopped
3 hard-boiled eggs
300 g (11 oz) tomatoes, quartered

1 Season the drained sauerkraut with walnut oil, vinegar, salt and pepper.

2 Add the chopped onion and parsley, and toss well to combine the ingredients. Arrange the hard-boiled eggs and tomatoes on top of the salad and serve.

SALADE DE POMMES DE TERRE ET HARENGS À L'HUILE
POTATO SALAD AND HERRINGS IN OIL

SERVES 6

1 kg (2¼ lb) potatoes
salt
2 tablespoons chives, chopped
400 g (14 oz) herring fillets in oil
100 g (4 oz) onions, peeled and finely sliced into rings
SAUCE VINAIGRETTE:
200 ml (⅓ pint) vegetable oil
6 tablespoons vinegar
salt and pepper
1 tablespoon made mustard

1 Cook the potatoes in their skins in boiling salted water. Allow to cool, then peel and dice. Whisk the vinaigrette ingredients together and add to the potatoes with the chives. Toss lightly.

2 Arrange the herring fillets and onion rings on top.

SALADE DE PISSENLITS AU MUNSTER GRATINÉ
DANDELION SALAD WITH MUNSTER TOASTS

SERVES 6

150 g (5 oz) smoked streaky bacon, diced
1 tablespoon oil
750 g (1½ lb) tender young dandelion leaves, washed
12 slices Munster cheese
12 slices French bread
300 g (11 oz) tomatoes, quartered
SAUCE VINAIGRETTE:
200 ml (⅓ pint) vegetable oil
6 tablespoons vinegar
salt and pepper

1 Fry the bacon gently in oil until crisp and golden brown.

2 Whisk the vinaigrette ingredients together and pour over the dandelion leaves. Add the hot bacon and toss.

3 Place a slice of Munster on each slice of bread and toast under the grill. Then arrange on top of the salad and garnish with quartered tomatoes.

SALADE DE CHOUX ROUGES AUX POMMES
RED CABBAGE WITH APPLES

SERVES 6

1 kg (2¼ lb) red cabbage, shredded
200 ml (⅓ pint) vinegar
6 tablespoons olive oil
salt and pepper
200 g (7 oz) dessert apples, peeled and cut in thin strips
50 g (2 oz) parsley, chopped

1 Place the shredded cabbage in a salad bowl. Bring the vinegar to the boil and pour over the cabbage. Toss well.

2 Season with oil, salt and pepper. Add the apples and parsley, and toss.

SALADE DE POMMES DE TERRE ET HARENGS À L'HUILE *(ABOVE)*
SALADE DE CHOUCROUTE À L'HUILE DE NOIX *(BELOW)*

SALADE DE CERVELAS *(ABOVE)*
SALADE DE CONCOMBRES À LA CRÈME *(BELOW)*

SALADE DE CERVELAS
CERVELAS SALAD

A cervelas is a smooth pork sausage originally made with brains – or cervelles *– hence the name. Large and lightly smoked, it is usually sold poached and can be eaten hot or cold.*

SERVES 6
6 poached cervelas
1 lettuce
100 g (4 oz) onions, peeled and finely chopped
Sauce Vinaigrette (see page 28), with the
addition of 2 tablespoons chopped parsley
3 hard-boiled eggs, quartered
500 g (1¼ lb) tomatoes, quartered

1 Cut the cervelas in half lengthwise and peel. Slash the rounded surface.

2 Line a salad bowl with a bed of lettuce and place the cervelas on top.

3 Add the onion and pour the vinaigrette over the top. Garnish with hard-boiled eggs and tomatoes.

CERVELAS AUX POMMES ET AU GRUYÈRE
CERVELAS WITH APPLES AND GRUYÈRE

SERVES 6
6 poached cervelas, peeled
300 g (11 oz) Gruyère
100 g (4 oz) dessert apples, peeled
2 tomatoes, quartered
Sauce Vinaigrette (see page 28)

1 Slice the cervelas finely widthways and then cut into *bâtonnets* or little sticks.

2 Also cut the Gruyère and apples into little sticks. Mix together all the ingredients in a bowl. Pour the vinaigrette over the salad and toss.

3 Arrange on a large flat dish and garnish with quartered tomatoes.

SALADE DE CERVELAS AUX CHOUX
CERVELAS SALAD WITH CABBAGE

SERVES 6
6 poached cervelas
500 g (1¼ lb) sauerkraut, rinsed in warm water
and drained
Sauce Vinaigrette (see page 28), with the
addition of 2 tablespoons chopped parsley
100 g (4 oz) onions, peeled and finely chopped
3 hard-boiled eggs, quartered
300 g (11 oz) tomatoes, quartered

1 Cut the cervelas in half lengthwise, peel and slash the rounded surface.

2 Line a salad bowl with half the sauerkraut and pour over half the vinaigrette. Place the cervelas on top. Sprinkle with chopped onion and add the remaining vinaigrette.

3 Garnish with hard-boiled eggs and tomatoes.

SALADE DE CONCOMBRES À LA CRÈME
CUCUMBER SALAD WITH CREAM

SERVES 6
2 small cucumbers, peeled and sliced
15 g (½ oz) salt
200 ml (⅓ pint) single cream
3 tablespoons white wine or cider vinegar
3 tablespoons chives, chopped

1 Sprinkle the slices of cucumber in a bowl with salt and leave to disgorge for 1 hour. Then take them out of the bowl, drain and squeeze to extract the moisture. Place in a salad bowl.

2 Season the cream with the vinegar and chives. Pour over the cucumber and marinate in the refrigerator for 1 hour. Serve very cold.

FISH AND SHELLFISH

Although Alsace is a land-bound region with no direct access to the sea, it suffers no shortage of fresh fish – salmon, trout, pike, carp, perch, bream and eel are all to be found in its rivers and ponds, and Alsatian cooks have evolved many ways of cooking these fish. Several varieties may be combined in white wine and stock to create *Matelote de Poissons*, or a single variety may be served in solitary splendour with perhaps only a cream sauce or buttered almonds as accompaniment, as in the trout recipes on page 38. *Quenelles de Brochet*, a classic method of cooking pike, are to be found in Alsace too, as are *écrevisses*, the little freshwater crayfish which Alsatian cooks poach simply in a wine stock and bring to table piled up in a serving dish.

MATELOTE DE POISSONS AU RIESLING
FISH STEW WITH RIESLING

This classic fish stew combines two Alsatian specialities – river fish and white wine – and is traditionally served with noodles.

SERVES 6 TO 8
500 g (1¼ lb) pike or carp, cleaned
500 g (1¼ lb) eels, skinned and cleaned
500 g (1¼ lb) perch, cleaned
500 g (1¼ lb) trout, cleaned
100 g (4 oz) shallots, peeled and finely chopped
200 g (7 oz) mushrooms, finely sliced
100 g (4 oz) butter
500 ml (18 fl oz) Riesling
1.5 litres (2½ pints) fish stock
salt and pepper
50 g (2 oz) flour
250 ml (8 fl oz) single cream
2 egg yolks
juice of 1 lemon
1 tablespoon chopped parsley

1 Cut the fish into pieces. Use the heads and tails to make fish stock.

2 Fry the shallots and mushrooms in half the butter but do not allow to brown. Add the Riesling, fish stock, salt and pepper. Poach the fish in this for about 10 minutes. (Trout and perch cook quicker than the other fish.)

3 Meanwhile, melt the remaining butter in a pan, stir in the flour and allow to cook, without colouring, for 2 or 3 minutes. Remove from the heat and allow to cool.

4 Remove the fish and the vegetables from the stock with a slotted spoon. Place in a dish, cover with aluminium foil and keep warm.

5 Add the stock to the mixture of flour and butter, stirring briskly with a whisk. Reduce for about 10 minutes.

6 Mix the cream, egg yolks and lemon juice together and pour into the well-reduced fish sauce. Check the seasoning and heat but do not allow to boil. While still very hot, pour over the fish and vegetables, and sprinkle with parsley. Serve the *matelote* immediately with noodles if liked (see page 64).

MATELOTE DE POISSONS AU RIESLING

Filets de Sandre Meunière *(ABOVE)*
Carpe à la Juive *(BELOW)*

CARPE À LA JUIVE
JEWISH-STYLE CARP

This famous regional dish has its origins in Alsace's Jewish heritage. It was intended for eating on the Sabbath because it could be prepared ahead and served cold, thereby avoiding cooking on the holy day, reserved for religious devotion.

SERVES 6 TO 8
2 × 1 kg (2 lb) carp
coarse salt
300 ml (½ pint) oil
2 medium onions, chopped
3 tablespoons finely chopped shallots
50 g (2 oz) flour
1 litre (1¾ pints) white wine
1 litre (1¾ pints) fish stock or water
4 cloves garlic, crushed
1 tablespoon chopped parsley
pepper

1 Clean the carp, removing the fins and scales but leaving both fish whole. Reserve the roe. Cut the fish into neat vertical slices about 1 cm (½ inch) thick, sprinkle with coarse salt and set aside for 15 minutes.

2 Rinse the fish slices under cold water and pat dry on paper towels. Heat 6 tablespoons of the oil in a large heavy-bottomed frying pan, add the onions and shallots and cook over moderate heat for 2 to 3 minutes until soft but not browned. Remove the vegetables from the pan, add the fish and the reserved roes and fry until cooked on all sides. With a fish slice, remove the slices of carp and keep warm.

3 Return the vegetables to the pan, sprinkle with the flour and cook for 2 minutes, then stir in the wine and fish stock. Add the garlic, half the parsley and pepper to taste. Bring to the boil, stirring, then reduce the heat, return the fish to the pan and simmer for 20 to 25 minutes.

4 Carefully transfer the slices of fish to a shallow dish and arrange in the form of the original fish. Sprinkle the remaining parsley over each 'fish'.

5 Bring the liquid in the frying pan to the boil and cook until reduced by two thirds. Whisk in the remaining oil. Pour the liquid over the fish, set aside to cook, then chill until required.

FILETS DE SANDRE MEUNIÈRE
FILETS OF PIKE-PERCH IN BUTTER

SERVES 6
3 × 575 g (1¼ lb) fresh pike-perch (or any firm white fish), heads removed and filleted
seasoned flour
50 g (2 oz) butter
2 tablespoons oil
2 tablespoons lemon juice
BEURRE NOISETTE:
100 g (4 oz) butter
2 tablespoons lemon juice
TO GARNISH:
1 lemon, peeled and cut in 6 slices
2 tablespoons chopped fresh parsley

1 Coat the fish in seasoned flour, shaking off the excess. Melt 50 g (2 oz) of the butter in the oil in a large frying pan. Add the fish and shallow-fry for 3 to 4 minutes on each side until golden brown.

2 Meanwhile, in a second pan, make the beurre noisette. Melt the butter over gentle heat. Allow it to brown, then stir in the lemon juice.

3 Transfer the cooked fish to a heated platter and sprinkle with the remaining lemon juice. Moisten with a little of the *beurre noisette* and top each fillet with a slice of lemon and a sprinkling of parsley. Serve immediately – the fish should be piping hot – with the remaining beurre noisette handed separately.

TRUITE FARCIE AU RIESLING
STUFFED TROUT WITH RIESLING

SERVES 6
100 g (4 oz) perch fillet
400 ml (14 fl oz) single cream
1 egg
salt and pepper
1 carrot, peeled and diced
1 leek, sliced
150 g (5 oz) celeriac, peeled and diced
100 g (4 oz) mushrooms, chopped
150 g (5 oz) butter
6×150-200 g (5-7 oz) trout
500 ml (18 fl oz) Riesling
500 ml (18 fl oz) fish stock
50 g (2 oz) shallots, peeled and chopped

1 Mince the perch and whisk in 6 tablespoons of cream, the egg, salt and pepper.

2 Cook the vegetables in 50 g (2 oz) butter, over a very gentle heat with the lid on the pan. Allow to cool and mix with the perch mixture.

3 Slit each trout along its backbone and carefully loosen the spine and bones, easing them and the entrails away from the flesh. Using scissors, cut through the spine just below the head and above the tail to release the bones. Wash the fish in cold water and pat dry with kitchen towels.

4 Sprinkle the trout with salt and stuff with the prepared mixture. Butter an ovenproof dish and add the salt, pepper, Riesling, fish stock and shallots. Lay the trout in the dish, cover with aluminium foil and bake in a moderate oven, at 180°C (350°F), Gas Mark 4, for about 20 minutes.

5 Skin the trout, leaving the head and tail intact, place in a buttered serving dish and keep hot. Strain the juice through a sieve, add the remaining cream and reduce by half. Thicken with the remaining butter and check the seasoning. Cover the trout with the hot sauce and serve.

TRUITE AUX AMANDES
TROUT WITH ALMONDS

SERVES 6
6×150-200 g (5-7 oz) trout
seasoned flour
175 g (6 oz) butter
75 g (3 oz) slivered almonds
lemon wedges, to garnish

1 Clean the trout, leaving the heads on. Wash, wipe dry and coat in seasoned flour.

2 Melt 100 g (4 oz) of the butter in a large frying pan. Add half the trout and cook over moderate heat for about 5 to 6 minutes until golden. To test whether the fish is done, press it lightly with a fork – the flesh should flake easily.

3 Using two fish slices or slotted spoons, transfer the fish to a heated platter. Keep warm while frying the remaining trout in the same way.

4 Add the remaining butter to the pan. When it sizzles, add the almonds. Cook over moderate to high heat, taking care that the butter does not burn and shaking the pan frequently, until the almonds are brown.

5 Spoon the hot almond and butter mixture over the trout and serve immediately, garnished with lemon wedges.

TRUITE FARCIE AU RIESLING

QUENELLES DE BROCHET AU GRATIN DE CHAMPIGNONS *(ABOVE)*
ANGUILLES AU PINOT NOIR EN FRICASSÉE D'OIGNONS *(BELOW)*

ANGUILLES AU PINOT NOIR EN FRICASSÉE D'OIGNONS
EELS WITH PINOT NOIR AND ONION FRICASSÉE

SERVES 6 TO 8
1.5 kg (3¾ lb) eels, skinned, cleaned and
thickly sliced
salt and pepper
6 tablespoons vinegar
100 g (4 oz) shallots, peeled and finely chopped
150 g (5 oz) butter
500 ml (18 fl oz) Pinot Noir
250 ml (8 fl oz) fish stock
150 ml (¼ pint) veal or chicken stock
500 g (1¼ lb) button onions, peeled
1 pinch of sugar
250 g (9 oz) mushrooms, quartered
juice of 1 lemon
6 thick slices white bread, cubed
1 tablespoon chopped parsley

1 Place the eels in a dish and sprinkle with salt and vinegar. Leave to marinate for 1 hour.

2 Gently fry the shallots in half the butter in a saucepan, then add the eels and allow to colour slightly. Deglaze with wine, add the fish and veal or chicken stock, season with salt and pepper and simmer, covered, for about 20 minutes.

3 Meanwhile, cook the onions in a pan with a little water (about 120 ml [4 fl oz]), sugar and a knob of butter. When they are soft, reduce the liquid and allow to brown. Then remove from the heat and reserve.

4 Fry the mushrooms gently in 25 g (1 oz) butter and put to one side.

5 Using a slotted spoon, place the eels in a dish and keep warm. Sprinkle with lemon juice. Reduce the remaining stock by half and check the seasoning. Fry the bread cubes in the remaining butter until golden brown.

6 Cover the eels with the hot sauce and add the reserved mushrooms and onions. Garnish with the *croûtons* and parsley.

QUENELLES DE BROCHET AU GRATIN DE CHAMPIGNONS
GRATINÉED PIKE QUENELLES WITH MUSHROOMS

SERVES 6 TO 8
800 g (1¾ lb) pike fillet
250 g (9 oz) butter
5 egg yolks
8 egg whites
salt and pepper
500 ml (18 fl oz) fish stock
500 ml (18 fl oz) single cream
100 g (4 oz) shallots, peeled and chopped
500 g (1¼ lb) mushrooms, finely chopped
juice of 1 lemon

1 Mince the pike fillet and beat in 200 g (7 oz) of the butter, 3 egg yolks and all the egg whites. Season with salt and pepper and leave for 1 hour in the refrigerator.

2 Meanwhile, mix the fish stock and 300 ml (½ pint) of the cream in a saucepan and reduce. Season with salt and pepper.

3 Fry the shallots gently in 25 g (1 oz) butter, add the mushrooms and lemon juice and simmer until all the mushroom liquor has evaporated. Put to one side.

4 Take the fish mixture out of the refrigerator and whisk in the remaining cream. Shape into *quenelles*, about 10 cm (4 inches) long. Poach in salted water for about 10 minutes. Drain and keep warm in an oven dish.

5 Mix 6 tablespoons of sauce with the 2 remaining egg yolks. Add the reserved mushrooms to the rest of the sauce, then add the mixture of egg yolks and sauce. Check the seasoning, pour over the *quenelles* and place under a hot grill to brown lightly. Serve immediately.

MOUSSELINE DE GRENOUILLES AU COULIS D'ÉCREVISSES
FROG'S LEG PÂTÉ WITH CRAYFISH SAUCE

SERVES 6

24 frogs' legs (sold in pairs, so 48 legs)
750 ml (1½ pints) fish stock or water
2 carrots, peeled and diced
1 leek, cleaned and sliced
100 g (4 oz) celeriac, diced
150 g (5 oz) butter
500 ml (18 fl oz) single cream
300 g (11 oz) pike or perch, skinned and boned
2 eggs
salt and pepper
450 g (1 lb) crayfish, fresh or frozen and thawed
6 tablespoons oil
6 tablespoons white wine
1 onion, peeled and sliced
1 tablespoon tomato purée
1 pinch of thyme
1 bay leaf
15 g (½ oz) flour

1 Poach the frog's legs in 250 ml (8 fl oz) fish stock. Remove from the stock, and bone. Dice the meat and put to one side.

2 Sweat half the diced carrot, a third of the sliced leeks and all the celeriac in 15 g (½ oz) butter. Add 6 tablespoons of cream and the frogs' leg stock. Reduce a little, then add the frogs' legs and continue simmering gently until almost dry. Allow to cool.

3 Mince the fish, add the eggs, salt, pepper and 75 g (3 oz) butter. Cool, stir in 200 ml (⅓ pint) cream, and sieve.

4 Butter six 150 ml (5 fl oz) ramekins and add half of the fish stuffing. Fill with a layer of the frogs' leg stew, then cover with the remaining fish stuffing.

5 To make the sauce, crush the crayfish and fry quickly in hot oil. Deglaze with a little of the white wine and add the remaining fish stock, the remaining carrot and leek, the onion, tomato purée, herbs and flour, and finally the remaining white wine. Season with salt and pepper, add the thyme and bay leaf and simmer for about 25 minutes.

6 Put the ramekins in a ovenproof dish with enough hot water to come halfway up the sides, and bake in a moderate oven, at 180°C (350°F), Gas Mark 4, for about 15 minutes.

7 Sieve the crayfish mixture, add the remaining cream and reduce by half. When the frogs' leg pâtés are cooked, demould on to a serving dish and keep warm. Thicken the crayfish sauce with the remaining butter and check the seasoning. Pour around the pâtés and serve.

COURT-BOUILLON D'ÉCREVISSES AU SYLVANER
CRAYFISH COURT-BOUILLON WITH SYLVANER

SERVES 6

100 g (4 oz) carrots, peeled and finely sliced
100 g (4 oz) leeks, finely sliced
100 g (4 oz) celeriac, peeled and finely sliced
100 g (4 oz) onion, peeled and finely sliced
1 litre (1¾ pints) Sylvaner
500 ml (18 fl oz) water
salt and pepper
1 pinch of thyme
1 bay leaf
1 pinch of chopped tarragon
48 crayfish, gutted
100 g (4 oz) butter
2 tablespoons chopped parsley

1 Place all the vegetables in a pan with the wine, water, salt, pepper, thyme, bay leaf and tarragon. Simmer gently for 1 hour.

2 Add the crayfish and poach for about 10 minutes. Transfer to a deep serving dish and keep warm.

3 Strain the *court-bouillon*, then reduce the stock by half. Gradually whisk in the butter to thicken the stock slightly (it should not be as thick as a sauce). Check the seasoning, pour over the crayfish and sprinkle with parsley.

COURT-BOUILLON D'ÉCREVISSES AU SYLVANER

MEAT DISHES

Alsatian food often demands robust appetites, and nowhere is this more evident than in the region's meat dishes. The best known, *Choucroute Garnie*, is an impressive combination of sauerkraut, potatoes, and meats. Lesser known, but almost as hearty, are hotpots such as *Potée Colmarienne* or *Bäckeofe*, a dish traditionally cooked in the baker's oven while the women were at the washplace.

PALETTE DE PORC À LA MOUTARDE
PORK SHOULDER WITH MUSTARD

SERVES 6
1 shoulder of pork weighing
1.5 kg (3¾ lb)
1 tablespoon made mustard
6 tablespoons oil
1 carrot, peeled and diced
1 onion, peeled and diced
1 leek, sliced
1 pinch of thyme
1 bay leaf
200 ml (⅓ pint) beef stock
150 g (5 oz) smoked streaky bacon, sliced and blanched
50 g (2 oz) goose fat or butter
1 kg (2¼ lb) green cabbage, sliced

1 Spread the pork with mustard and brown in a casserole with oil. Add the carrot, onion, leek and herbs, and pour over the beef stock and a little water to cover. Put the casserole in a preheated moderate oven, at 180°C (350°F), Gas Mark 4, and cook for 1½ hours, basting frequently.

2 Fry the bacon in goose fat or butter, add the cabbage and simmer gently, covered, for 30 minutes. Add a glass of water if it becomes a little dry.

3 The meat is cooked when a skewer plunged into it comes out hot. Remove from the casserole. Strain the cooking juices through a sieve and reduce if necessary to make a sauce. Check the seasoning. Slice the pork and serve with the cabbage and the sauce.

QUENELLES DE FOIE AUX OIGNONS ET CROÛTONS
LIVER QUENELLES WITH CROÛTONS

SERVES 6
1 onion, peeled and chopped
2 cloves garlic, peeled and crushed
100 g (4 oz) parsley, chopped
150 g (5 oz) butter
300 g (11 oz) pork liver or young ox liver
150 g (5 oz) smoked streaky bacon
100 g (4 oz) bread, with crusts cut off
25 g (1 oz) flour
4 eggs
salt and pepper
grated nutmeg
150 g (5 oz) onions, peeled and sliced
100 g (4 oz) *croûtons*

1 Fry the chopped onion, garlic and half the parsley in 50 g (2 oz) butter.

2 Mince together the liver, bacon and bread. Stir in the onion, garlic, parsley, flour and eggs, and season with salt, pepper and nutmeg.

3 Shape into fat sausages with the help of two soup spoons, and poach in simmering salted water for 10 minutes.

4 Meanwhile, sweat the sliced onions in the remaining butter and brown lightly. Add the *croûtons* and brown.

5 Remove the *quenelles* from the water and arrange on a serving dish. Place the onions and *croûtons* on top and sprinkle with the remaining parsley. Serve very hot.

Q̨UENELLES DE FOIE AUX OIGNONS ET CROÛTONS *(ABOVE)*
PALETTE DE PORC À LA MOUTARDE *(BELOW)*

BÄCKEOFE

JAMBONNEAU DE PORC AUX LENTILLES
PORK KNUCKLES WITH LENTILS

SERVES 4 TO 6
2 knuckles of ham
100 g (4 oz) carrots, peeled and diced
100 g (4 oz) leeks, cleaned and chopped
100 g (4 oz) celery, diced
75 g (3 oz) goose fat or butter
500 g (1¼ lb) green or brown lentils, soaked
overnight
1 pinch of thyme
1 bay leaf
1 onion, peeled
5 cloves
salt and pepper
2 cloves garlic
100 g (4 oz) tomatoes, diced
COURT-BOUILLON:
1 carrot, peeled and sliced
1 onion, peeled and sliced
1 stick celery
1 leek
1 pinch of thyme
1 bay leaf

1 Place the knuckles of ham and the ingredients for the *court-bouillon* in a large saucepan. Bring to the boil and simmer for 1½ hours.

2 Sweat the carrots, leeks and celery in goose fat or butter, add the lentils, thyme and bay leaf, and the onion studded with cloves. Add some of the *court-bouillon* and simmer for 45 minutes.

3 Check that the lentils are cooked. Season with salt and pepper and add the garlic and tomatoes. Cook for another 10 minutes. Carve the knuckles into slices and serve with the lentils.

BÄCKEOFE
MEAT AND POTATO HOTPOT

SERVES 6
500 g (1¼ lb) shoulder of lamb, cubed
500 g (1¼ lb) silverside or shoulder of beef,
cubed
500 g (1¼ lb) neck or shoulder of pork, cubed
300 g (11 oz) onions, peeled and finely sliced
200 g (7 oz) leeks, sliced
500 ml (18 fl oz) Riesling
1 pinch of thyme
2 bay leaves
2 cloves garlic, peeled and crushed
100 g (4 oz) goose fat or butter
1.5 kg (3¾ lb) potatoes, peeled and thickly
sliced
salt and pepper
2 pig's trotters (optional)
100 g (4 oz) flour

1 Place all the meat in a bowl with the onions, leeks and wine. Add the herbs and garlic and leave to marinate, covered, in the refrigerator overnight.

2 The following day, drain the meat and reserve the marinade. Grease a 1.5 litre (2½ pint) casserole dish with goose fat or butter and arrange half the potato slices on the bottom. Cover with the marinated meat, onions and leeks. Season with salt and pepper. Place the remaining slices of potato on top and add the reserved marinade and a little water to cover. Place the pig's trotters on top (if using).

3 Make a soft dough with the flour and a little water. Cover the dish with the lid and seal the edges with this dough.

4 Bake in a moderate oven, at 180°C (350°F), Gas Mark 4, for 2½ hours. Serve very hot, straight from the dish.

CHOUCROUTE GARNIE ALSACIENNE
ALSATIAN-STYLE SAUERKRAUT

SERVES 8 TO 10

2 onions, peeled and finely sliced
100 g (4 oz) goose fat or butter
500 ml (18 fl oz) Riesling
500 ml (18 fl oz) water
2 cloves garlic, peeled and chopped
1 pinch of thyme
2 bay leaves
10 juniper berries
3 cloves
3 knuckles of salt pork
300 g (11 oz) smoked streaky bacon
1 kg (2¼ lb) salt pork loin
2 kg (4½ lb) raw sauerkraut, rinsed in warm water
1.5 kg (3¾ lb) medium potatoes, peeled
salt
6 Quenelles de Foie (see page 44)
6 Strasbourg sausages, scored with a sharp knife
300 g (11 oz) *boudins blancs*

1 Sweat the onions in goose fat or butter and do not allow to brown. Add the wine and water, garlic, thyme, bay leaves, juniper berries and cloves, and bring to the boil. Then add the pork knuckles, bacon and pork loin and place the sauerkraut on top. Do not add salt. Cover with a lid and simmer gently for 1½ hours, checking from time to time that there is some liquid in the pot.

2 When everything is cooked, place the potatoes to steam on top of the sauerkraut. Bring some slightly salted water to the boil and poach the liver *quenelles* and the Strasbourg sausages for 10 minutes. Poach the *boudins blancs* and keep warm.

3 When the sauerkraut and potatoes are cooked, place the sauerkraut in a warm, deep serving dish. Arrange the bacon, pork knuckles and pork loin, cut into pieces, on top. Surround with liver quenelles, potatoes, Strasbourg sausages and *boudins blancs*. Serve very hot on warm plates.

PIÈCE DE BOEUF BRAISÉE AU PINOT NOIR
BRAISED BEEF WITH PINOT NOIR

SERVES 6

1.5 kg (3¾ lb) topside of beef
500 ml (18 fl oz) Pinot Noir
1 onion, peeled and sliced
1 carrot, peeled and sliced
2 cloves garlic, peeled and crushed
1 stick celery, sliced
6 tablespoons oil
1 litre (1¾ pints) beef stock
1 pinch of thyme
1 bay leaf
salt and pepper
50 g (2 oz) butter

1 Place the beef in a bowl with the wine and all the vegetables and leave to marinate in the refrigerator for 24 hours.

2 Drain the meat and pat dry, reserving the marinade. Brown the meat in oil in a casserole and add the vegetables and the reserved marinade. Cover with the stock and add the thyme, bay leaf, salt and pepper. Place the lid on top and cook slowly in a cool oven, at 150°C (300°F), Gas Mark 2, for 3 hours.

3 Check that the beef is cooked. Remove from the casserole and keep warm. Reduce the cooking juices, thicken with butter and check the seasoning. Cut the meat into slices and serve the juices separately in a sauceboat.

CHOUCROUTE GARNIE ALSACIENNE

POT-AU-FEU AU RAIFORT

POT-AU-FEU AU RAIFORT
POT-AU-FEU WITH HORSERADISH

SERVES 8
1.5 kg (3 lb) stewing beef
1 oxtail
coarse salt
20 peppercorns
1 large onion, stuck with 4 cloves
3 cloves garlic, peeled
1 small bunch parsley
pinch of thyme
3 bay leaves
4 medium carrots, peeled and roughly chopped
2 medium turnips, peeled and cut into quarters
450 g (1 lb) leeks, washed and tied into a bunch
1 bulb celeriac, peeled and diced or 1 head
celery, thickly sliced
6 marrow bones
2 large potatoes, peeled and cut into quarters
300 ml (½ pint) crème fraîche
200 g (7 oz) grated horseradish
gherkins, to serve

1 Place the beef and the oxtail in a large saucepan. Add water to cover. Stir in 1 tablespoon coarse salt with the peppercorns, onion, garlic and herbs. Bring to the boil.

2 When the water boils, skim off any scum that has risen to the surface, then add the carrots, turnips, leeks, celeriac or celery. Cover the pan, and simmer for 1¾ hours.

3 Rub the marrow bones with coarse salt. Add them to the pan with the potatoes and simmer for about 20 minutes more. Adjust the seasoning and check that the beef and vegetables are cooked. Remove the excess fat from the surface of the stock.

4 Strain 500 ml (18 fl oz) of the defatted stock into a clean saucepan, add the crème fraîche and cook over a high heat until reduced by half. Stir in the horseradish.

5 Remove the meat from the saucepan, slice and serve on a heated dish. Serve the drained vegetables in a second dish and hand the sauce separately, with gherkins and a bowl of coarse salt as accompaniments.

POTÉE COLMARIENNE (SÜRI RÜEWE)
COLMAR HOTPOT

SERVES 6
1.5 kg (3 lb) turnips
salt
75 g (3 oz) butter
2 tablespoons oil
2 large onions, finely chopped
2 cloves garlic, crushed
450 g (1 lb) smoked blade of pork or forehock
bacon, cubed
2 pork or veal knuckles
300 ml (½ pint) Alsace Riesling or Pinot Blanc
300-450 ml (½-¾ pint) water

1 Peel and thinly slice the turnips. Spread them out in a shallow dish, sprinkle with salt and set aside for 1 hour. Transfer the slices to a colander, wash well, and remove excess water by pressing the slices against the sides of the colander with a wooden spoon.

2 Melt the butter in the oil in a large heavy-bottomed saucepan. Add the onions and garlic. Sauté for 3 to 4 minutes until the onion is transparent. Add a layer of half the turnips to the pan, then add the meat. Top with the remaining turnips. Pour over the wine and 300 ml (½ pint) of the water.

3 Bring the liquids to the boil. Cover the pan tightly, lower the heat and simmer for 1½ to 2 hours. Check the pan occasionally and add the rest of the water if necessary.

4 Remove the pork knuckles from the pan and cut the meat from the bone. To serve, pile the turnip mixture on a heated serving platter, with the meat in the centre.

POULTRY AND GAME

Alsace enjoys a wide variety of poultry and game, and these are combined with other local produce to create a number of delicious dishes. Chicken may be cooked in Riesling or quail with grapes, for instance, while Alsatian beer features in *Fricassée de Lapin à la Bière*. The most impressive dish of all, though, must be *Faisan en Chartreuse* on page 59 – sliced pheasant layered in a mould of vegetables.

COQ AU RIESLING
CHICKEN CASSEROLE WITH RIESLING

SERVES 4 TO 6
1 × 1.5 kg (3¾ lb) roasting chicken, jointed
150 g (5 oz) butter
100 g (4 oz) shallots, peeled and chopped
25 g (1 oz) flour
250 ml (8 fl oz) Riesling
1 clove garlic, peeled and crushed
1 pinch of thyme
1 bay leaf
250 ml (8 fl oz) chicken stock
salt and pepper
300 g (11 oz) mushrooms, sliced
juice of 1 lemon
250 ml (8 fl oz) single cream
2 tablespoons chopped parsley

1 Gently fry the pieces of chicken in a casserole with 50 g (2 oz) of the butter. Add the shallots and fry for 1 or 2 minutes, then add the flour and fry for another 1 or 2 minutes. Deglaze with wine and add the garlic, thyme, bay leaf and stock. Season with salt and pepper, cover and simmer for 30 minutes.

2 Meanwhile, moisten the mushrooms with a little water and add the lemon juice and 25 g (1 oz) butter. Cook until soft, then strain the cooking juices into the casserole.

3 Transfer the cooked chicken to a deep serving dish, with the mushrooms, and keep warm. Strain the cooking juices through a sieve, add the cream and reduce for 10 minutes. Whisk in the remaining butter, and check the seasoning. Pour the hot sauce over the chicken and sprinkle with chopped parsley.

FRICASSÉE DE LAPIN À LA BIÈRE
RABBIT CASSEROLE WITH BEER

SERVES 6 TO 8
1.75 kg (4 lb) rabbit, jointed
100 g (4 oz) smoked bacon, sliced
100 g (4 oz) butter
50 g (2 oz) shallots, peeled and chopped
1 clove garlic, peeled and chopped
500 ml (18 fl oz) beer
6 tablespoons chicken stock
salt and pepper
1 pinch of thyme
1 bay leaf
200 g (7 oz) pickling onions, peeled
1 pinch of sugar
25 g (1 oz) butter
200 ml (⅓ pint) single cream
2 tablespoons chopped parsley

1 Fry the rabbit and bacon in half the butter in a casserole and allow to brown slightly. Add the shallots and garlic and fry for a few minutes longer. Deglaze with beer and add the stock, salt, pepper, thyme and bay leaf. Cover and simmer for 45 minutes to 1 hour.

2 Blanch the onions, then sweat in the butter and sugar until just golden.

3 Transfer the rabbit to a serving dish and keep warm. Pour the cream into the cooking juices and reduce by half. Check the seasoning and stir in the remaining butter. Pour the sauce over the rabbit. Garnish with the prepared onions and sprinkle with chopped parsley.

COQ AU RIESLING *(ABOVE)*
FRICASSÉE DE LAPIN À LA BIÈRE *(BELOW)*

CIVET DE LIÈVRE

CIVET DE LIÈVRE (HASEPFEFFER)
HARE STEW

SERVES 6 TO 8
225 g (8 oz) unsmoked bacon, diced
1.75 kg (4 lb) hare, jointed, blood and liver
reserved
salt and pepper
1 teaspoon dried thyme
1 bay leaf
3 onions, sliced
4 tablespoons olive oil
2 tablespoons Marc d'Alsace or brandy
50 g (2 oz) butter
18 shallots, peeled
18 button mushrooms, wiped
1 clove garlic, crushed
25 g (1 oz) plain flour
350 ml (12 fl oz) red wine
350 ml (12 fl oz) game or beef stock
bouquet garni
5 tablespoons single cream
parsley sprigs, to garnish

1 Bring a small saucepan of water to the boil. Add the bacon and cook for 2 minutes. Drain and reserve.

2 Put the hare in a shallow dish and season with salt, pepper and thyme. Add the bay leaf and 1 of the sliced onions. Combine the oil and brandy in a small bowl. Mix well and pour over the hare. Turn the joints until well coated in the marinade and set aside for 2½ to 3 hours.

3 Melt half the butter in a large frying pan. Add the bacon cubes and sauté gently until golden brown. With a slotted spoon, remove the bacon and reserve. Add the shallots to the butter remaining in the pan and sauté for 4 to 5 minutes. Remove and reserve. Repeat the procedure with the mushrooms, removing them from the pan after 2 minutes.

4 Add the remaining butter to the pan. Stir in the remaining sliced onions and the crushed garlic, and sauté for 4 to 5 minutes until golden brown. Add the flour and cook until golden, stirring constantly.

5 Drain the hare, reserving the marinade, and pat the joints dry on paper towels. Add them to the roux and cook, stirring constantly, until browned. Pour over the red wine and stock, stir thoroughly and add the bouquet garni. Bring the liquid to the boil, lower the heat and simmer the hare for 1 to 1¼ hours until the meat is tender.

6 Transfer the hare to a flameproof casserole and add the reserved bacon, shallots and mushrooms. Add the reserved marinade to the saucepan in which the hare was simmered and mix well to combine all the ingredients. Strain the contents of the saucepan into the casserole.

7 Cover the casserole and cook in a preheated moderate oven, at 180°C (350°F), Gas Mark 4 for 1 hour. About 10 minutes before serving, chop the reserved liver and stir it into the casserole. Place the casserole over moderate heat.

8 Mix the reserved blood with the cream and add it to the casserole. Cook, stirring constantly, for about 8 minutes. Do not allow the sauce to boil. Serve garnished with parsley. Noodles (see page 64) are the traditional accompaniment to *Civet de Lièvre*.

CANARD BRAISÉ FARCI AUX POMMES
BRAISED DUCK WITH APPLE STUFFING

SERVES 4 TO 6
2 kg (4½ lb) duck
1 large carrot, peeled and roughly chopped
1 leek, roughly chopped
2 stalks celery, cut in 5 cm (2 inch) lengths
1 onion, roughly chopped
2 tomatoes, skinned and roughly chopped
1 bay leaf
2 sprigs of thyme
250 ml (8 fl oz) white wine
250 ml (8 fl oz) water
STUFFING:
50 g (2 oz) butter
1 small onion, chopped
1 cooking apple, peeled, cored and diced
75 g (3 oz) duck or chicken livers, finely
chopped
100 g (4 oz) pork sausagemeat
100 g (4 oz) soft white breadcrumbs
2 tablespoons chopped parsley
1-2 tablespoons Calvados or brandy
salt and pepper
grated nutmeg

1 Prepare the stuffing: melt the butter in a frying pan, add the onion and cook for 2 to 3 minutes until golden. Add the duck livers and cook for about 2 minutes. Transfer the mixture to a bowl and add the apples, sausagemeat, breadcrumbs and parsley. Stir well. Moisten with Calvados and add salt and pepper and nutmeg to taste. The stuffing should be fairly firm.

2 Wipe the duck inside and out with absorbent kitchen paper and pull out the loose fat around the neck and inside the body. Stuff the body cavity loosely and truss the bird.

3 Place the duck in a roasting pan and cook in a preheated hot oven at 220°C (425°F), Gas Mark 7 for 30 minutes. Carefully transfer the duck to a platter and pour off all but 1 tablespoon of the fat from the roasting pan.

4 Add the carrot, leek, celery, onion and tomatoes to the roasting pan, stirring well. Place the duck on top of the vegetables and bury the bay leaf and thyme in the mixture. Pour over the wine and water.

5 Reduce the oven temperature to moderate, 180°C (350°F), Gas Mark 4, and cook for 1½ hours more, basting the duck with the pan juices every 15 minutes and removing excess fat from the pan.

6 When cooked, remove the duck to a heated serving platter. Strain the cooking juices into a saucepan, skim off the fat from the surface and bring the liquid to the boil. Cook, stirring, until reduced by half, then pour into a sauceboat and serve with the duck. Braised red cabbage makes an excellent accompaniment (see page 60).

CAILLES AUX RAISINS
QUAIL WITH GRAPES

SERVES 6
6 quail
salt and pepper
100 g (4 oz) butter
50 g (2 oz) shallots, peeled and chopped
200 g (7 oz) grapes, peeled and seeded
3 tablespoons brandy
3 tablespoons white wine
6 tablespoons beef stock

1 Season the quail with salt and pepper and truss. Brown all over in a casserole with half the butter. Place the casserole in a moderately hot oven, at 200°C (400°F) Gas Mark 6, for 10 minutes to finish cooking the quail.

2 Transfer the quail to a serving dish, remove the string and keep warm.

3 Fry the shallots in the casserole in the remaining butter and add the grapes. Deglaze with brandy and wine, add the stock and reduce for a few minutes. Pour over the sauce and serve.

CANARD BRAISÉ FARCI AUX POMMES

Faisan en chartreuse

FAISAN EN CHARTREUSE
CHARTREUSE OF PHEASANT

This traditional chartreuse of pheasant is time-consuming to prepare, but beautiful in appearance and exquisite in taste – a truly impressive dish for a grand occasion.

SERVES 6

150 g (5 oz) butter
1 oven-ready hen pheasant
1 large green cabbage, outer leaves removed and cored
1 tablespoon lard or dripping
225 g (8 oz) lean bacon, rinds removed and reserved
1 large onion, chopped
1 litre (1¾ pints) game or beef stock
1 bouquet garni
225 g (8 oz) *Saucisses de Morteau*, chipolata sausages or bacon
175 g (6 oz) white turnips, peeled and cut into 4 cm (1½ inch) sticks
175 g (6 oz) carrots, peeled and cut into 4 cm (1½ inch) sticks
175 g (6 oz) French beans, topped, tailed and cut in half
salt and pepper

1 Heat the oven to moderately hot, 200°C (400°F) Gas Mark 6. Melt 100 g (4 oz) of the butter in a roasting pan on top of the stove. Add the pheasant and baste all over with the butter. Transfer the pan to the oven and cook for 15 minutes.

2 Meanwhile bring a large saucepan of water to the boil. Add the cabbage and cook for 10 minutes. Drain, separate the leaves and set aside to cool while you cook the bacon rinds and onion.

3 Melt the lard in a large heavy-bottomed saucepan. Add the bacon rinds with the onion and cook lightly for 4 to 5 minutes until the onion is golden. Add a layer of half the cabbage. Top with the pheasant and bacon rashers. Cover with the remaining cabbage leaves, moisten with the stock and add the bouquet garni. Bring the liquid to the boil, lower the heat and cook for 1 hour. Add the sausages and cook for 30 minutes.

4 While the pheasant is cooking, bring a saucepan of lightly salted water to the boil. Add the turnip and cook for 2 minutes. With a slotted spoon, transfer the turnips to a small bowl. Repeat the procedure with the carrots and beans, but cook the beans for 4 to 5 minutes. Keep all the vegetables separate.

5 When the pheasant is cooked, remove it from the pan and cut the flesh into neat slices. Reserve the sausages and bacon. Place the cabbage leaves in a colander and press with a wooden spoon to extract as much liquid as possible.

6 Assemble the chartreuse: with the remaining butter, thickly grease a 2 litre (3½ pint) chartreuse mould or pudding basin. Line the inside of the mould with turnip and carrot sticks, pressing them into the butter in horizontal layers and adding layers of beans for contrast.

7 Line the base and sides of the prepared mould with cabbage leaves and add the pheasant. Top with the remaining cabbage, pressing the mixture well down into the mould. Season with salt and pepper. Cover with a circle of buttered greaseproof paper.

8 Place the mould in a roasting pan half filled with boiling water and bake in a preheated moderate oven, at 180°C (350°F), Gas Mark 4 for 30 minutes. Return the sausages and bacon to the oven for the last 10 minutes to reheat.

9 Allow the mould to stand for 5 minutes. Remove the paper and invert the chartreuse on to a heated serving platter. Slice two of the sausages in rounds to garnish the top and surround the chartreuse with the remaining sausages and the bacon. Serve at once.

VEGETABLES AND NOODLES

Although vegetables do not feature greatly in Alsatian cuisine, there are a number of regional vegetable dishes. Cabbage – the basis of *choucroute* – is of course a favourite, and there are special recipes for kohlrabi, potatoes and asparagus. The Alsatians also make their own noodles – crisply fried *spätzele* or soft *nouilles fraîches* – which are never served on their own in the Italian fashion, but provide the traditional accompaniment to other dishes, notably poultry and game.

CHOUX ROUGES BRAISÉS AUX POMMES
BRAISED RED CABBAGE WITH APPLES

SERVES 6 TO 8
1 large red cabbage, thinly sliced
salt and pepper
2 carrots, peeled and diced
1 leek, chopped
100 g (4 oz) celeriac, peeled and diced
1 clove garlic, peeled and chopped
1 onion, peeled and chopped
100 g (4 oz) butter
6 tablespoons vinegar
500 ml (18 fl oz) red wine
200 ml (⅓ pint) veal or chicken stock
1 pinch of thyme
1 bay leaf
150 g (5 oz) dessert apples, finely sliced

1 Blanch the cabbage in boiling salted water and drain.

2 Sweat the remaining vegetables in butter in an ovenproof casserole and deglaze with vinegar and red wine. Add the veal or chicken stock and bring to the boil. Season with salt and pepper, add the thyme and bay leaf and then the cabbage. Cover with a lid and cook in a moderately hot oven, at 200°C (400°F), Gas Mark 6, for 30 minutes.

3 Add the apples and cook for a further 10 minutes.

4 At the end of the cooking time, check that the cabbage is cooked. If the cooking juices are too thin, reduce in a pan to the desired quantity – the cabbage will be all the better for this. Check the seasoning and serve hot with a meat dish, such as Palette de Porc à la Moutarde (see page 44), or duck (see page 56).

CHOUX-RAVES À LA CRÈME
KOHLRABI WITH CREAM

SERVES 6
1.5 kg (3¾ lb) kohlrabi, finely sliced
300 ml (½ pint) single cream
6 tablespoons chicken stock
salt and pepper
grated nutmeg
1 tablespoon chopped *fines herbes* (such as parsley, tarragon, chives, chervil)

1 Cook the kohlrabi in boiling salted water, cool and drain.

2 Combine the cream and stock and reduce by half. Season with salt, pepper and grated nutmeg and add the *fines herbes*.

3 Mix the kohlrabi with the sauce, bring to the boil and serve very hot.

CHOUX-RAVES À LA CRÈME *(ABOVE)*
CHOUX ROUGES BRAISÉS AUX POMMES *(BELOW)*

GALETTES DE POMMES DE TERRE

CHOUX FARCIS AU FOIE GRAS
CABBAGE STUFFED WITH GOOSE LIVER

SERVES 6 TO 8
1 large green cabbage
salt and pepper
250 g (9 oz) veal
250 g (9 oz) lean pork
300 g (11 oz) pork fat
150 g (5 oz) *foie gras* (fattened goose or duck
liver)
2 eggs
6 tablespoons single cream
2 carrots, peeled and diced
1 leek, chopped
150 g (5 oz) celeriac, peeled and diced
200 g (7 oz) smoked bacon, diced
100 g (4 oz) butter
1 litre (1¾ pints) veal or chicken stock
1 pinch of thyme
1 bay leaf
1 clove garlic, peeled and crushed

1 Separate the cabbage leaves individually and blanch in salted boiling water. Refresh under cold water and drain on a dry cloth.

2 Mince the veal, pork, pork fat and liver. Beat the eggs and mix with the cream. Stir the eggs and cream into the meat mixture, and season with salt and pepper.

3 Sweat the carrots, leek, celeriac and the smoked bacon in butter and place in a deep ovenproof dish.

4 Place a spoonful of the stuffing mixture on each cabbage leaf and gather the edges to form cabbage parcels, squeezing lightly in the palm of the hand. Continue in this way until all the cabbage leaves and stuffing has been used.

5 Lay the cabbage parcels on top of the vegetables in the ovenproof dish. Cover with the stock and add the thyme, bay leaf and crushed clove of garlic. Cover the dish with greaseproof paper or a tightly fitting lid and bake in a moderately hot oven, at 200°C (400°F), Gas Mark 6, for 35 to 40 minutes.

6 Transfer the stuffed cabbage to a serving dish and keep warm. Reduce the cooking juices as necessary and pour over the stuffed cabbage. Serve very hot.

GALETTES DE POMMES DE TERRE (GRUMBEEREKIECHLE)
POTATO CAKES

SERVES 4 TO 6
1 kg (2¼ lb) potatoes, peeled and grated
3 eggs
100 g (4 oz) onions, peeled and chopped
1 tablespoon flour
1 tablespoon chopped parsley and chives
1 clove garlic, peeled and crushed
salt and pepper
grated nutmeg
6 tablespoons oil

1 Place the peeled and grated potatoes in a sieve and rinse well under cold running water. Drain well and place in a bowl. Mix in the eggs, onion, flour, herbs and garlic. Season with salt, pepper and nutmeg and stir thoroughly.

2 Heat the oil in a frying pan. Shape the prepared mixture into small cakes with a spoon and fry on both sides, making sure they are well coloured. Serve very hot as an accompaniment to a meat dish, or on its own as a lunch or supper dish with a well-seasoned green salad and some charcuterie.

GRATIN D'ASPERGES AU JAMBON
GRATINÉED ASPARAGUS AND HAM

SERVES 6
1 kg (2¼ lb) asparagus, trimmed
salt
juice of 1 lemon
1 teaspoon sugar
300 ml (½ pint) single cream
200 ml (⅓ pint) chicken stock
salt and pepper
grated nutmeg
6 slices boiled ham
15 g (½ oz) butter
100 g (4 oz) grated cheese

1 Cook the asparagus for 15 to 20 minutes in boiling salted water acidulated with lemon juice and sweetened with sugar, until just firm. Cool in the cooking water.

2 Combine the cream and stock and reduce by half. Season with salt, pepper and a little grated nutmeg.

3 Drain the asparagus and roll in the slices of boiled ham. Arrange in a buttered ovenproof dish. Cover with the well-reduced cream, sprinkle with grated cheese and brown in a moderately hot oven, at 200°C (400°F), Gas Mark 6, for about 25 minutes.

SPÄTZELE
FRIED PASTA

SERVES 6 TO 8
1 kg (2¼ lb) flour
10 eggs
6 tablespoons milk
salt and pepper
grated nutmeg
4 litres (7 pints) water
15 g (½ oz) cooking salt
1 tablespoon oil
100 g (4 oz) butter, for frying

1 Sift the flour into a bowl and make a well in the centre. Add the eggs and milk, and gradually incorporate these into the flour. Season with salt, pepper and a pinch of grated nutmeg. Work with a wooden spoon until the dough is smooth but not too thick. Allow to rest for about 15 minutes.

2 Bring the water to the boil with the salt and oil.

3 Place a sieve over the saucepan of boiling water, making sure that the water does not touch the bottom of the sieve. Pour some of the dough into the sieve and press through the holes with the palm of your hand. As small balls of pasta rise to the surface of the boiling water, remove with a slotted spoon and cool in cold water. Repeat the process until all the dough has been used.

4 Drain the *spätzele* and fry in butter. Serve immediately, while still very hot, with a meat dish, such as venison.

NOUILLES FRAÎCHES
FRESH NOODLES

SERVES 6 TO 8
575 g (1¼ lb) flour
1 teaspoon salt
grated nutmeg
6 eggs
6 tablespoons water
1 tablespoon oil

1 Sift the flour into a bowl and mix in the salt and nutmeg. Gradually work in the eggs and the water. Roll into a ball and allow to rest in a cool place for 1 hour.

2 Shape the dough into 5 or 6 balls and roll with a rolling pin until they are 3 mm (⅛ inch) thick. Sprinkle with flour and roll into cigar shapes. Using a sharp knife, cut into strips about 1 cm (½ inch) wide.

3 Cook the noodles in boiling salted water to which you have added a little oil. Drain and serve very hot as the traditional accompaniment to meat, poultry or game.

GRATIN D'ASPERGES AU JAMBON

DESSERTS AND BAKING

Apples, cherries, *quetsch* and *mirabelle* plums – these are just some of the many fruits grown in Alsace's orchards, so it is no surprise to learn that the fruit tarts of Alsace are renowned. Fruit is also used to make fritters, another speciality and, echoing its German past, the region also produces several varieties of biscuit, cake and sweet bread. The best known is the distinctively shaped and brioche-like *Kügelhopf*, a fruity loaf eaten for breakfast or in the afternoon with a glass of wine.

TARTE AU FROMAGE BLANC
CHEESECAKE

SERVES 6
25 g (1 oz) raisins, soaked in
1 tablespoon Kirsch
250 g (9 oz) Pâte Brisée (see page 77)
200 g (7 oz) *fromage blanc*
3 tablespoons single cream
100 g (4 oz) sugar
3 eggs, separated
15 g (½ oz) potato flour or arrowroot
zest of 1 lemon, grated
25 g (1 oz) icing sugar

1 Line a 23 cm (9 inch) loose-bottomed flan tin with shortcrust pastry. Prick the bottom with a fork.

2 Place the *fromage blanc* in a bowl and mix with the cream and sugar. Incorporate the egg yolks and potato flour, and add the lemon zest. Beat the egg whites until stiff and fold gently into the cream cheese mixture. Pour into the shortcrust pastry case and sprinkle the surface with the soaked raisins.

3 Bake in a moderate oven, at 180°C (350°F), Gas Mark 4, for 10 minutes. Lower the temperature to 150°C (300°F), Gas Mark 2, and bake for a further 40 minutes. The cheesecake is cooked when the blade of a knife plunged into it comes out dry.

4 Take out of the oven, remove from the tin and allow to cool. When cold, dust with icing sugar.

TARTE AUX POMMES ALSACIENNE
APPLE TART ALSACE-STYLE

SERVES 6 TO 8
25 g (1 oz) butter
250 g (9 oz) Pâte Brisée (see page 77)
1 kg (2¼ lb) Golden Delicious or green dessert apples, peeled, cored and quartered
150 g (5 oz) caster sugar
1 teaspoon ground cinnamon
3 tablespoons milk
150 ml (¼ pint) single cream
2 eggs
25 g (1 oz) icing sugar

1 Butter a 25 cm (10 inch) loose-bottomed flan tin and line with shortcrust pastry. Prick the bottom with a fork.

2 Slice the quartered apples without separating the slices and spread out fan-fashion on the base of the tart. Sprinkle with 25 g (1 oz) of the caster sugar and the cinnamon. Bake in a preheated oven at 200°C (400°F), Gas Mark 6 for 20 to 25 minutes.

3 Mix the remaining sugar in a bowl with the milk, cream and eggs. Pour over the cooked apples. Return to the oven for a further 10 to 15 minutes.

4 When the tart is cooked, dust with icing sugar and serve warm.

TARTE AUX POMMES ALSACIENNE *(ABOVE RIGHT)*
TARTE AU FROMAGE BLANC *(BELOW)*

Kügelhopf

TARTE À LA RHUBARBE
RHUBARB TART

SERVES 6 TO 8
500 g (1¼ lb) rhubarb, chopped
150 g (5 oz) caster sugar
25 g (1 oz) butter
250 g (9 oz) Pâte Brisée (see page 77)
2 eggs
250 ml (8 fl oz) single cream
25 g (1 oz) icing sugar

1 Sprinkle the rhubarb with 50 g (2 oz) of the caster sugar and allow to stand for 30 minutes.

2 Butter a 25 cm (10 inch) loose-bottomed flan tin and line with short-crust pastry. Drain the rhubarb and spread over the pastry case. Bake in a preheated oven at 200°C (400°F), Gas Mark 6 for 15 minutes.

3 Mix the eggs, the remaining caster sugar and the cream in a bowl. Pour this over the rhubarb and bake for a further 10 minutes at 180°C (350°F), Gas Mark 4.

4 When the tart is cooked, dust with icing sugar and serve warm.

TARTE AUX QUETSCHES À LA CANNELLE
DAMSON TART WITH CINNAMON

SERVES 6 TO 8
25 g (1 oz) butter
250 g (9 oz) Pâte Brisée (see page 77)
1 egg white, lightly beaten
2 or 3 plain biscuits, crushed
1 kg (2 lb) damsons or small red plums, stoned and halved
100 g (4 oz) caster sugar
15 g (½ oz) cinnamon
15 g (½ oz) icing sugar

1 Butter a 25 cm (10 inch) loose-bottomed flan tin and line with shortcrust pastry. Prick the bottom with a fork and brush with egg white. Sprinkle the base of the tart with broken biscuits and arrange the damsons on top. Mix together the caster sugar and cinnamon and sprinkle over the fruit.

2 Bake in a preheated, moderately hot oven, at 200°C (400°F), Gas Mark 6, for about 30 minutes.

3 Remove from the oven, dust with icing sugar, and serve.

KÜGELHOPF
KIRSCH AND RAISIN LOAF WITH ALMONDS

MAKES 1 LARGE LOAF
250 ml (8 fl oz) milk
100 g (4 oz) sugar
25 g (1 oz) yeast
750 g (1½ lb) flour
1 pinch of salt
3 eggs
150 g (5 oz) butter, softened
50 g (2 oz) raisins, soaked in
3 tablespoons Kirsch
25 g (1 oz) almonds, whole
25 g (1 oz) icing sugar

1 Warm the milk with 25 g (1 oz) sugar and dissolve the yeast in it. Sift the flour, remaining sugar and salt into a bowl, reserving a very little flour. Stir in the milk and yeast mixture. Add the eggs to the dough and knead. Incorporate the butter and continue kneading until the dough comes away easily from your hands. Then gather it all together in the bowl, sprinkle with the reserved flour, cover with a damp cloth and allow to prove in a warm place for 1 hour, until doubled in volume. When risen, incorporate the raisins and Kirsch.

2 Butter a *kügelhopf* mould. Line the bottom with almonds, place the dough on top and allow to rest until it reaches the edges of the mould. Bake in a preheated, moderate oven at 180°C (350°F), Gas Mark 4 for 40 minutes. If the loaf becomes too brown, cover with aluminium foil. The loaf is cooked when it makes a sharp dry sound when you tap it. Turn out, cool on a wire rack and dust with icing sugar.

PÂTE À BEIGNETS
FRITTER BATTER

MAKES 300 ML (½ PINT)
250 g (9 oz) plain flour
6 eggs, separated
6 tablespoons light beer or lager
200 ml (⅓ pint) water
25 g (1 oz) sugar

1 Sift the flour into a mixing bowl, make a well in the centre and place the egg yolks, beer and water in the well. Gradually incorporate these into the flour, stirring all the time to avoid lumps. Add the sugar and allow to rest in a cool place for 30 minutes.

2 Whisk the egg whites stiffly and fold gently into the batter. Use to coat slices of any firm fruit, such as apples or pears. Deep-fry the fritters, drain on kitchen towels, dredge with caster sugar, and serve.

BEIGNETS DE CARNAVAL
CARNIVAL FRITTERS

SERVES 6 TO 8
500 g (1¼ lb) plain flour
250 ml (8 fl oz) milk
15 g (½ oz) yeast
4 eggs
75 g (3 oz) caster sugar
100 g (4 oz) butter, softened
6 tablespoons Kirsch
oil for deep frying
25 g (1 oz) cinnamon

1 Sift the flour into a bowl. Heat the milk gently and dissolve the yeast. Mix into the flour, add 50 g (2 oz) of the sugar, the butter and Kirsch. Allow to rest for 1 hour.

2 Roll the dough until about 5 mm (¼ inch) thick. Cut into shapes and fry in very hot oil until golden brown.

3 Remove from the pan and drain. Sprinkle lightly with the remaining sugar and cinnamon.

SORBET AUX FRAMBOISES
RASPBERRY SORBET

SERVES 6 TO 8
400 ml (14 fl oz) water
400 g (14 oz) sugar
450 g (1 lb) raspberries, puréed
juice of 1 lemon
1 egg white, whisked

1 Bring the water and sugar to the boil and boil for 1 minute. Pour the syrup into a bowl and allow to cool.

2 Combine the raspberry purée, syrup and lemon juice. Strain through a sieve into a freezing container and leave to half-freeze to a mushy consistency. Turn the half-frozen mixture into a bowl and fold in the egg white, mixing thoroughly. Return to the container and re-freeze.

3 Remove the sorbet from the freezer when it reaches the desired consistency, and serve.

SORBET AU MARC DE GEWÜRZTRAMINER
BOOZY SORBET

SERVES 6 TO 8
600 ml (1 pint) water
400 g (14 oz) sugar
200 ml (⅓ pint) Gewürztraminer Marc
juice of 2 lemons
1 egg white, whisked

1 Bring the water and sugar to the boil and boil for 1 minute. Allow to cool. Add the Marc and lemon juice.

2 Pour into a freezing container and leave to half-freeze to a mushy consistency. Turn the half-frozen mixture into a bowl and fold in the egg white, mixing thoroughly. Return to the container and re-freeze.

3 Remove from the freezer when it reaches the desired consistency.

BEIGNETS DE CARNAVAL *(ABOVE)*
SORBET AU MARC DE GEWÜRZTRAMINER *(BELOW)*

TARTE FLEURIE *(ABOVE)*
PETITS FOURS DE NOËL *(BELOW)*

TARTE FLEURIE (STREUSELKÜECHE)
CRUMBLE CAKE

SERVES 8 TO 10
400 g (14 oz) plain flour
¼ teaspoon salt
15 g (½ oz) fresh yeast
6-8 tablespoons milk
50 g (2 oz) butter
4 tablespoons caster sugar
1 egg, beaten
2 tablespoons apricot jam
STREUSEL:
125 g (4½ oz) plain flour
50 g (2 oz) sugar
pinch of cinnamon
100 g (4 oz) butter, diced

1 Sift the flour and salt into a large mixing bowl. Mash the yeast in a second bowl. Place 6 tablespoons of the milk in a small saucepan and heat to lukewarm. Add butter and stir until melted, then add to the yeast, stirring until dissolved. Beat in the sugar and egg.

2 Make a well in the flour, add the milk mixture and mix until smooth, adding more milk if necessary, until a firm dough is formed. When the dough comes away from the sides of the bowl, tip it on to a floured surface and knead until smooth and elastic.

3 Place the dough in a greased bowl, cover with a damp cloth and set aside to rise for 50 minutes or until doubled in bulk. Knock the dough down, reshape, cover and allow to rise again, either for about 30 minutes in a warm place, or overnight in the refrigerator.

4 To shape the dough, roll it out to a thickness of about 2.5 cm (1 inch) and pat to a round. Place in a lightly greased 23 cm (9 inch) deep pie dish or cake tin. Cover and set aside to rise again for about 30 minutes.

5 Meanwhile make the streusel: combine the flour, sugar and cinnamon in a bowl. Rub in the butter with your fingers to form a crumble. Heat the oven to moderately hot, 190°C (375°F), Gas Mark 5.

6 Warm the apricot jam and spread it over the surface of the dough. Add a generous layer of streusel and bake in the middle of the oven for 45 minutes, until the cake is golden and a skewer inserted through the side to the centre comes out clean. Cool on a wire rack.

PETIT FOURS DE NOËL (SCHWOWEBRETLE)
CHRISTMAS PETIT FOURS

MAKES ABOUT 36
350 g (12 oz) plain flour
225 g (8 oz) butter
225 g (8 oz) caster sugar
225 g (8 oz) ground almonds
2-3 egg yolks
1 teaspoon mixed spice
75 g (3 oz) preserved orange peel or mixed peel, chopped
50 g (2 oz) currants
1 teaspoon finely grated lemon rind
beaten egg, to glaze

1 Sift the flour and form into a circle on a floured work surface.

2 Cream the butter with the sugar in a bowl. Stir in the almonds. Add two of the egg yolks, one at a time, beating well after each addition. Mix in the spice, chopped peel, currants and lemon rind.

3 Place the almond mixture in the centre of the flour and knead until all the ingredients are amalgamated to a firm dough. Add the third egg yolk if necessary. Set the dough aside to harden for 1 hour. Heat the oven to moderate, 180°C (350°F), Gas Mark 4.

4 Roll out the dough to a thickness of 3 mm (⅛ inch) and cut out fancy shapes with pastry cutters. Place on buttered baking sheets, brush lightly with beaten egg and bake for 10 to 15 minutes until golden. Allow to cool slightly, then transfer to wire racks to cool.

BIREWECKE
DRIED FRUIT LOAF

MAKES 1 LARGE LOAF
350 g (12 oz) plain flour
pinch of salt
90-120 ml (3-4 fl oz) milk
50 g (2 oz) butter
15 g (½ oz) fresh yeast or 7 g (¼ oz) dried yeast
50 g (2 oz) caster sugar
1 egg, beaten
150 g (5 oz) dried figs, cut into strips
150 g (5 oz) stoned prunes, cut into strips
150 g (5 oz) dried pears, cut into strips
100 g (4 oz) raisins
100 g (4 oz) currants
2 tablespoons roughly chopped hazelnuts
8 walnuts, roughly chopped
1 teaspoon kirsch
1 teaspoon grated lemon rind
1 teaspoon freshly grated nutmeg
egg yolk to glaze

1 Sift the flour and salt into a large bowl. Pour 90 ml (3 fl oz) of the milk into a saucepan and heat to lukewarm. Add the butter and stir until melted.

2 Pour the warm milk on to the yeast and mash until dissolved. (If using dried yeast, follow packet instructions.) Stir in the sugar and beaten egg.

3 Make a well in the flour and add the milk mixture. Stir until smooth, adding more warm milk if necessary to form a pliable dough. Knead until smooth.

4 Place the dough in a greased bowl. Cover and leave in a warm place until doubled in bulk (about 1-1½ hours). While the dough is rising, mix the dried fruit and nuts with the kirsch.

5 Knock down the dough and work in the dried fruit mixture, with the lemon rind and nutmeg. Shape the dough into an oval and place on a lightly greased baking sheet. Allow to rise for 1 hour more.

6 Brush the loaf with egg yolk to glaze and bake in a preheated hot oven, 200°C (400°F), Gas Mark 6 for 10 minutes, then reduce the temperature to moderate, 180°C (350°F), Gas Mark 4 and bake for 30 to 40 minutes more until the loaf sounds hollow when rapped on the base.

PETITS FOURS À L'ANIS (ANISBRETLE)
SMALL ANISEED COOKIES

MAKES ABOUT 48
3 eggs
225 g (8 oz) sugar
1 tablespoon aniseed
300 g (11 oz) plain flour

1 Beat the eggs and sugar in a large bowl until the mixture is thick and pale and forms folds.

2 Add the aniseed and flour, stirring to form a fairly thick dough.

3 Drop spoonfuls of the dough on to a lightly greased baking sheet, leaving space between each for spreading. Leave to dry for 24 hours.

4 Bake in a preheated moderate oven, 180°C (350°F), Gas Mark 4 for about 10 minutes. The tops of the cookies should be pale and well risen, the bottoms golden brown. Cool slightly, then transfer from the baking sheet to a wire rack and cool completely.

PETITS FOURS A L'ANIS *(ABOVE)*
BIREWECKE *(BELOW)*

PÂTE FEUILLETÉE

PÂTE BRISÉE
SHORTCRUST PASTRY

MAKES 300 G (11 OZ)
250 g (9 oz) plain flour
75 g (3 oz) butter, cut into small pieces
1 egg
1 pinch of salt
6 tablespoons water
50 g (2 oz) sugar (optional)

1 Sift the flour into a bowl. Rub the butter into it between finger and thumb of both hands until the mixture resembles fine breadcrumbs, or work to the crumb stage in a food processor, being careful not to overmix.

2 Add the egg, salt, water and sugar (if used) and mix quickly until it forms a ball of dough. Allow to rest for 15 minutes before use or wrap in polythene and keep in the refrigerator for 1 or 2 days until required.

PÂTÉ À PÂTÉS EN CROÛTE
HOT-WATER CRUST PASTRY FOR *EN CROÛTE PÂTÉS*

MAKES 450 G (1 LB)
120 g (4½ oz) lard, cut into small pieces
3 tablespoons boiling water
375 g (13 oz) plain flour
1 egg

1 Melt the lard in the water. Sift the flour and salt into a mixing bowl and add the melted lard and egg.

2 Quickly beat with a wooden spoon to form a fairly soft dough and shape into a ball. Cover with plastic film or a damp tea towel and allow to rest in the refrigerator for at least 20 to 30 minutes or until required.

PÂTE FEUILLETÉE
FLAKY PASTRY

MAKES 550 G (1¼ LB)
400 g (14 oz) plain flour, sifted
200 ml (⅓ pint) water
2 teaspoons salt
300 g (11 oz) butter, diced

1 Make a well in the flour and into it pour the water and salt. Mix well and knead until the dough is smooth. Form the dough into a ball and leave to stand for about 30 minutes.

2 Roll out the dough to a rough square, keeping the centre part thicker than the edges. Place the diced butter in the middle and flatten lightly with the palm of the hand.

3 Fold the sides of the dough into the centre to enclose the butter. Roll out the dough to a rectangle three times as long as it is wide. Continue to roll until you can see the butter through the dough, but stop before it breaks the surface. Fold the rectangle in three (first turn). Allow the dough to rest for 15 minutes.

4 Give the dough a quarter turn, roll out and fold as before. Allow to rest for 15 minutes.

5 Repeat the process four times more, giving the dough a quarter turn each time and allowing it to rest for 15 minutes at each stage to give a total of six turns. The pastry is now ready for use.

INDEX